Content-Focused Coaching[SM]

Content-Focused Coaching^{SM}

Transforming
Mathematics Lessons

Lucy West
Fritz C. Staub

HEINEMANN   UNIVERSITY OF PITTSBURGH
Portsmouth, NH   Pittsburgh, PA

Heinemann
A division of Reed Elsevier Inc.
361 Hanover Street
Portsmouth, NH 03801–3912
www.heinemann.com

University of Pittsburgh
3939 O'Hare Street
Pittsburgh, PA 15260
www.pitt.edu

Offices and agents throughout the world

Content-Focused Coaching[SM] is a service mark of the University of Pittsburgh, through its Learning Research and Development Center.

The authors and publishers wish to thank those who have generously given permission to reprint borrowed material:

Figures 1–2, 1–3, 1–4, and Appendix 1 are reprinted by permission of the Learning Research and Development Center, University of Pittsburgh.

"Eleven Fruits" from *Mathematical Thinking in Grade 1* by Marlene Kliman, Susan Jo Russell, Tracey Wright, and Jan Mokros. Copyright © 1998 by Dale Seymour Publications. Reprinted by permission of Pearson Education, Inc.

continued on p. v

Library of Congress Cataloging-in-Publication Data
West, Lucy.
    Content-focused coaching : transforming mathematics lessons /
Lucy West, Fritz Staub.
        p.   cm.
    Includes bibliographical references.
    ISBN 0-325-00462-5 (acid-free paper)
    1. Mathematics—Study and teaching (Elementary).   2. Teachers,
Training of.   3. Mathematics—Study and teaching (Elementary)—
New York (State)—New York—Case studies.   4. Teachers, Training
of—New York (State)—New York—Case studies.   I. Staub, Fritz.
II. Title.
QA135.6 .W47 2003
372.7—dc21   2002190847

Editor: Victoria Merecki
Production editor: Sonja S. Chapman
Cover design: Jenny Jensen Greenleaf
Cover photo: Christina Santiago
Compositor: House of Equations, Inc.
Manufacturing: Steve Bernier

Printed in the United States of America on acid-free paper
07 06 05 04   VP   4 5

continued from p. iv

"Combining Fractions in a Design" from *Investigations, Grade 4* by Cornelia Tierney, Mark Ogonowski, Andee Rubin, and Susan Jo Russell. Copyright © 1998 by Dale Seymour Publications. Reprinted by permission of Pearson Education, Inc.

"Brownies" from *Investigations in Number, Data, and Space: Fair Shares* by Cornelia Tierney and Mary Berle-Carman. Copyright © 1998 by Dale Seymour Publications. Reprinted by permission of Pearson Education, Inc.

All video footage is used by permission of the Learning Research and Development Center, University of Pittsburgh.

The authors wish to give special thanks to:

The United States National Science Foundation Grant ESI9731424, the Swiss National Science Foundation Fellowship 8210–037090, New York City's Community School District 2, the High-Performance Learning Communities project at Learning Research and Development Center (LRDC) under the Office of Educational Research and Improvement (OERI) contract RC 96–1327002 and NetLearn, at Learning Research and Development Center, funded by a Technology Innovation Challenge Grant from the U.S. Department of Education. Any opinions, findings, and conclusions expressed in this material are those of the authors and do not necessarily reflect the views of the Swiss National Science Foundation, the United States National Science Foundation, the LRDC, or the OERI.

Contents

Foreword

It would not be surprising for the general public to come across images in a newspaper, on a television show, or in a weekly news magazine of two physicians, or two lawyers, or two architects huddled together talking about a patient, a court case, or designs for a new construction site. It is rare, however, for the public to see images of two teachers lost in conversation about a new course of study, a particular lesson, or the performance of a group of students. Perhaps, it would be even more surprising for noneducators to discover that one of those teachers, the one with more expertise in a particular subject area, is coaching his or her colleague, helping the less-accomplished teacher become a more effective one.

In this book, *Content-Focused Coaching*SM, the authors Lucy West and Fritz Staub help us understand how such collaboration is not only possible, they demonstrate why such frequent, scholarly, and well-designed "meetings of minds" is essential, if educators are to rise to the ranks of the well-respected professional across this country and throughout the world.

As the superintendent of a large urban school district in New York City, there are many reasons why I will be recommending this book to a wide range of colleagues, including staff developers, teachers, principals, and superintendents. First and foremost, Lucy and Fritz demonstrate how Content-Focused Coaching, a clear, manageable, and precise staff development structure, can prevent teachers from becoming technicians by providing them with the confidence and know-how to maintain themselves as decision makers. In other words, Lucy and Fritz reveal practical ways for teachers to become more thoughtful, deliberate, and essentially smarter about the work they do. Theirs is no touchy-feely, loosey-goosey mentoring approach, but rather a rigorous and respectful system for guiding and supporting teachers as they go about making changes in their teaching. Certainly, in these days of high attrition rates for teachers it becomes essential to wrap teachers in the kinds of support that keeps them energized, passionate, and informed about their fields of study and well equipped to help all of their students succeed. Content-Focused Coaching is just such a support system.

Then too, the authors have raised the bar when it comes to knowing what high-quality staff development looks, feels, and sounds like. Using the teaching of mathematics as their centerpiece, they help us understand why staff development must be content-rich and site-specific. It must also involve time for meticulous co-planning and thoughtful reflection. Through accompanying CDs, as well as through transcripts of coaching conversations and teaching moments, the authors cut off the tops of their heads and let us look inside, demonstrating how such teaching essentials as knowing content deeply, carefully preparing the teaching environment, anticipating students' responses, following students' lines of thinking, asking probing questions, and making other deliberate teaching moves can help students acquire difficult concepts and increase their academic performance. Throughout, the authors demonstrate how the qualities of honesty and clarity strengthen their abilities to coach well, but it should also be noted that these qualities are present in their writing, making this text an accessible and essential resource for all those involved in the professional development of teachers. Although steeped in the mathematics arena, West and Staub's big ideas have implications for all teaching and learning interactions including staff development in literacy, science, and social studies.

Of course, this book also provides the reader with opportunities to view constructivist mathematics teaching in action. The descriptions of the planning and teaching moments are so detailed and engaging that together with the accompanying CDs, readers will feel like Kathy, Dave, and Katherine are teaching just down their hallways. Certainly these brief teaching glimpses will leave the reader hungering for more information about the *Investigations* curriculum, with increased understanding of what it means to teach number sense, fractions, and division. So too, the reader will find themselves jotting notes about the role of curriculum materials, the use of blackboard space, and the importance of continually asking oneself, "What is the mathematics in this lesson?" Above all, teachers will long to have the kind of professional company that Lucy and Fritz describe.

Additionally, *Content-Focused Coaching* is a must-read for principals who are determined to live up to their roles as instructional leaders. The authors provide administrators with much food for thought concerning the meaning of pedagogical content knowledge, the look and sound of a well-designed lesson, the search for evidence in student learning, the need for professional collegiality, and the roles staff developers can play in the life of a school. For those administrators who have been attempting to apply the Principles of Learning to their schoolhouses (a framework developed by Lauren Resnick and colleagues at the University of Pittsburgh), this book will illustrate clearly how those principles support best practice in teaching and learning. Such concepts as Accountable Talk, Socializing Intelligence, and Clear Expectations are woven into each staffroom conversation and classroom scene. As Lucy processes her coaching moments, she highlights how those principles have informed her staff development work and improved the mathematics instruction in the classrooms she knows best.

Finally, and most personally, I am incredibly privileged to write a foreword for *Content-Focused Coaching*, because so much of the research that forms the basis of this work took place in the district that I call home. Lucy West, in collaboration with Fritz Staub and alongside an incredible staff of mathematics coaches and teacher leaders, has revolutionized the teaching of mathematics in Community School District 2 in New York City. This incredible team has empowered and enabled thousands of educators to know what it means to think mathematically, to share the finest of mathematical teaching with their students, and to understand how the art of Content-Focused Coaching has enabled them to reach glorious professional heights. Our school district is forever in their debt.

—Shelley Harwayne

Foreword

There has probably never been a more challenging time for educators. More is expected of them and the stakes are higher than ever. All children, not just a privileged few, are to be taught a high-demand curriculum with, ideally, an expectation of understanding and thoughtful performance. And, just as the expectations for students are pushing teachers into uncharted territory, accountability systems in some places seem to be making unrealistic demands.

At the same time, more is understood about how both children and adults learn, and powerful new systems of instruction are being created to help teachers meet their new professional demands. We know, for example, that understanding of complex concepts in mathematics and other fields is within reach of all children, but that understanding develops in uneven and individual "bursts" that require patient teaching and continuous student effort. We know how well crafted combinations of student activities and guided talk work to build knowledge and understanding. We know that posing questions that help students reason things out for themselves and directly teaching important information and concepts are not conflicting philosophies of education, but rather twin essential elements in a powerful process of assisted learning. Finally, we know that intelligence and aptitude for learning can be created through targeted effort, and that students' identities as learners are intertwined with their specific learning efforts and activities.

Achieving a balance between imparting fundamental knowledge and teaching processes for using and even creating that knowledge is perhaps teachers' greatest challenge. Good thinking is impossible without a solid core of knowledge. Yet learning basic facts and concepts requires using one's mind. So we can't teach the facts first and let thinking follow any more than we can teach thinking first and let the facts come later. Academic rigor and the thinking curriculum need to be part of the same package, not—as some have proposed—an either-or proposition.

All of this takes us well the beyond mathematics of our childhood—unless we were among a small minority who learned the subject from a mentor rather than from a textbook. Research and practical experience show that our children can meet these new expectations if they have the opportunity to learn a rigorous mathematics curriculum under the guidance of expert teachers—teachers who understand fundamental mathematics concepts, know how to establish tasks and ask questions that engage students in grappling with these concepts, and are skilled at interpreting students' responses. A smaller but equally convincing body of research and experience shows that teachers too are up to the challenge—if they are offered the opportunity to learn the craft under the guidance of skilled mentors.

Enter the promise of coaching. No one expects an athlete or a musician to become great without a coach—an over-the-shoulder mentor who pushes and supports, watches and intervenes at critical moments, analyzes learners' actions and challenges them to become self-critical analysts of their own performances. Just so with teaching. It is a demanding craft, requiring of its practitioners both careful planning and finely tuned adaptation to the flow of classroom activity and conversation. The craft can be learned, but not from a textbook. It must be learned through guided practice.

The idea of coaching for teachers is not new. But the concept of *content-focused* coaching is. If the heart of powerful learning is combining deep knowledge with powerful thinking, then coaching must be focused squarely on the specific knowledge to be taught and learned. General principles and friendly questions are not enough to produce the kinds of mathematics instruction that today's standards and expectations call for. The effective math teaching coach must know the mathematics in depth and be able to show teachers how to set specific learning goals for a lesson, devise or select powerful tasks, analyze the knowledge—correct and "misconceived"—that children are likely to bring to the tasks, and plan instructional conversations that are contingent on student responses and hence open to improvisation.

Content-Focused Coaching is part of a broad movement away from drill and recitation as the primary mode of education. But it is *not* generic "constructivism" of the kind that nudges educators away from focusing on the knowledge that students are to acquire or advises against telling students anything directly. We might say that Content-Focused Coaching is about *knowledge-based* constructivism. Or, alternatively, it is about intellectually engaged *in*structivism. Either way, it is something new in the world of teaching.

It gives me great personal pleasure to see this book on Content-Focused Coaching in mathematics come to fruition. Throughout a career first as a scholar of learning and then as an education reform "activist," I have been fortunate to be surrounded by colleagues who have taught me how constructivism and instructivism can work together. Two such individuals came together at the Institute for Learning in Pittsburgh in the late 1990s. Lucy West, an artist of mathematics instruction, was building a coaching system for teachers in Community District 2 in New York City. At the same time, Fritz Staub—a visiting postdoctoral student who became an international fellow of the Institute when he returned to Europe—brought the Swiss tradition of deep subject matter analysis by teachers to our learning community. Others, including Donna Bickel who was developing a program for literacy coaches, joined the conversation.

The fusion of research and practice in the Institute for Learning provided a nurturing setting for these conversations. The extraordinary environment of District 2, where continuous learning was expected of everyone and supported in a series of "nested learning communities," provided a setting in which details of coaching practice could be molded into shape. Here is the result, a theoretically grounded yet practical manual for coaches of mathematics teachers, and a vision of the possible for American public schools. Enjoy it. Use it. Watch the lights go on in your teachers' and children's eyes.

—Lauren B. Resnick

Acknowledgments

The authors of this book met at the Institute for Learning in 1995 and began an unusual collaboration between researcher and practitioner. Our ongoing interaction has sculpted the practice of Content-Focused Coaching in teaching elementary and middle school mathematics in Community School District 2, New York City. Content-Focused Coaching is grounded in a conceptual framework developed by Fritz C. Staub in interaction with the Institute for Learning at the Learning Research and Development Center, University of Pittsburgh, and with Community School District 2. The Institute for Learning continues to use this professional development model in mathematics and is currently working on applying this framework to other subject matter areas.

The development of the practice of Content-Focused Coaching in District 2 would not have been possible without the cooperation and support of many people. The professional learning community fostered by the visionary and supportive leadership of Anthony Alvarado, superintendent; Elaine Fink, deputy superintendent; and Bea Johnstone, assistant superintendent, provided fertile ground for Content-Focused Coaching. Many principals and teachers were eager to work with the mathematics staff developers as we ventured into the complex and demanding task of improving mathematics instruction for all students. A special thank-you goes to Anna Switzer, principal of Public School 234, who served as personal mentor and friend to Lucy West and opened the school's doors to the mathematics initiative from its very first days. Her leadership and support were unwavering. Anna Marie Carrillo, principal of Public School 116, provided greatly appreciated encouragement, support, and innovative leadership in the change process. Thanks also to Alice Young, principal of Intermediate School 131, for sharing her insights and enthusiasm. We acknowledge and appreciate the insights and encouragement of Elizabeth Gewirtzman. We offer heartfelt gratitude to Kathy Sillman, Dave Younkin, and Katherine Casey, the three teachers who generously allowed us to use their work as case studies in this book. We consider them to be exemplary dedicated teaching professionals.

A special thank-you goes to the mathematics staff developers and technology staff in Community School District 2 who played a key role in the implementation and refinement of Content-Focused Coaching, without whom there would be no Mathematics Initiative in the district. Each and every one of them generously shared their wisdom, their skills, and their insights with us. Without the technology support provided by Lynel Kantor, we literally would not have been able to complete this book, which to a large extent was written via email message between Switzerland and New York. Thank you Ginger Hanlon, Susan Picker, Gary Shevell, Deborah Flaum, Christina Santiago, and Anne Samartine for taking added responsibilities and keeping the Mathematics Initiative in full swing. Thanks, Elizabeth Sweeney, Charlene Marchese, Suzanne Werner, Sarah Ryan, Deborah Altenau, Deborah Flaum, and Linda Methnetsky, for allowing us to use your voices in the last chapter. Thanks to all of the mathematics staff developers who incorporated Content-Focused Coaching into their practice and kept us informed of how it played out in the field. In particular we would like to thank Sandra Nye, Elizabeth Sweeney, Sarah Ryan, Nina Liu, Jean Risolo, Joan Backer, Karen Cardinali, Kerry Cunningham, Charlene Marchese, Phyllis Tam, Monica Witt, Toni Cameron, Kate Abell, Kevin Tallat-Kelpsa, Anne Burgunder, Jennifer DiBrienza, Maggie Siena, Brenda Strassfeld, Christine Calliandro, and Ronald Feinstein. Jennifer Li provided invaluable clerical support.

Thanks also to Nicholas Branca for his assistance in making the mathematics portions of the text reader friendly.

Thanks to Shelley Harwayne, superintendent, District 2, for her encouragement, and for her foreword to this book.

We extend deep gratitude to Lauren B. Resnick, the founder and director of the University of Pittsburgh's Institute for Learning, for her vision, her guidance, her support of our work, and her foreword.

We recognize the contributions of Victoria Bill, a resident fellow at the Institute for Learning, and Andrea Miller, a professional developer in the Monaca, Pennsylvania, school district, who were the first to collaborate with Fritz C. Staub and to use the emerging conceptual frame and tools of Content-Focused Coaching for professional development in elementary mathematics. We greatly appreciate their collaboration, encouragement, and feedback, which have been instrumental in the development of this model. During the 2001–2002 school year, the Institute for Learning worked with the school districts of Sharon, Pennsylvania, and South Beaver, Pennsylvania, under the leadership of Victoria Bill, to implement Content-Focused Coaching in elementary mathematics.

The initial collaboration between Fritz C. Staub and the Institute for Learning was made possible by a fellowship of the Swiss National Science Foundation and an invitation from Lauren Resnick to work as a visiting scholar at the University of Pittsburgh's Learning Research and Development Center. Since 1997 the University of Pittsburgh has provided the funding and the University of Zürich/Switzerland has made available additional resources that have made it possible to continue this collaboration across cultures and between practice and research.

We are also grateful for the vision and financial support of the United States National Science Foundation and in particular to Diane Spresser, Anna Suarez, and Skip Fennel.

In 1999 Donna DiPrima Bickel, a resident fellow at the Institute for Learning, began to use and develop strategies to implement the framework and tools of Content-Focused Coaching as a professional development model in elementary literacy. During the 2000–2001 school year, she developed a course with Nancy Artz to train thirty elementary literacy coaches in Providence, Rhode Island. During the 2001–2002 school year, she and three other resident fellows at the Institute for Learning, Donna Micheaux, Annette Seitz, and Lillie Sipp, worked with the school districts of Austin, Texas, Los Angeles, California, and Providence, Rhode Island, to implement the Content-Focused Coaching model in elementary literacy. Our collaboration with Donna Bickel helped to refine the communication of the general framework of Content-Focused Coaching and her work began to broaden its application to a different subject area. To honor this collaboration and her help in editing Chapter One, "What Is Content-Focused Coaching?" we acknowledge Donna as coauthor of that chapter. We are also grateful for Donna's leadership and support in arranging for high-quality videotaping of coaching sessions in District 2, which two of the CDs included in this book are based on. The video material for the third CD has been recorded as part of the High-Performance Learning Communities (HPLC) project at the Learning Research and Development Center (LRDC) under Office of Educational Research and Improvement (OERI) research contract, which studied the work in Community School District 2. We are grateful to HPLC for allowing us to use this document as an example of the practice of Content-Focused Coaching. For the editing of the videos we were fortunate to have someone as competent and keen as Luise Caster, of the NetLearn project, at the Learning Research and Development Center.

We are indebted to Nancy Israel, the executive associate director of the Institute for Learning, for her leadership and support in solving the organizational and legal issues to make this book a reality.

We thank Alan Huisman for his editorial help in making the first chapter reader friendly despite its theoretical content. Finally, enormous thanks to Victoria Merecki. You are the most patient, caring, and encouraging editor, and for sure we couldn't have done it without you.

Preface

Education is undergoing profound and challenging changes. An increasingly complex world has high and often conflicting expectations for the knowledge and skills to be acquired by students in schools. These expectations have caused some educators to flee the profession, others to dig their heels in and proclaim allegiance to tradition, and still others to open to a world of possibilities. Content-Focused Coaching is a professional development model designed to assist educators to engage in thoughtful dialogues that result in improved teaching and learning—dialogues that can rekindle a passion for meeting the challenges of teaching. In Content-Focused Coaching, teacher and coach collaboratively plan, teach, and reflect upon classroom lessons. This collaboration is designed to provide teachers with individualized, adaptive, and situation-specific assistance focused on content, pedagogy, and student learning.

Becoming and being a wonderful and effective teacher is an ongoing, career-long process. Sustainable improvement requires more than superficial changes in methods, the adoption of a new curriculum program, or the latest educational jargon. It requires changes in one's underlying knowledge base and beliefs, coupled with time to understand and implement those beliefs. Over the past three decades, new theoretical developments and a vast field of highly specific empirical research on learning and teaching have led to new ways of thinking about student learning and teachers' roles. Yet this research and the actual practice of teaching have too often been disconnected. Researchers leave it up to practitioners to make sense of and apply the vast number of highly specific findings. Practitioners tend to remain captured in their personal experience and the demands of local settings in which time for and access to research is limited.

We think it is the role of educators, as members of a professional community, to keep abreast of the research about how students learn and consider its implications for best teaching practices. The road from theory to practice runs through highly complex terrain and is often long and uncharted. We assume that all teachers can *learn* to be effective, empowering educators—there is no teacher gene. Teaching is a learnable craft—it takes effort, support, deep and flexible content knowledge, a large repertoire of learning strategies and teaching methods, and basic understanding of theories of learning. We take the stance that professional dialogue on learning and teaching at the school site, in relation to particular students, in specific academic domains, is necessary for developing successful and replicable practices of teaching. We envision teachers engaging in frequent professional conversations with colleagues and researchers. Content-Focused Coaching is a vehicle for teachers to continue to become smarter about teaching and learning and to develop, share, and refine best practices. Content-Focused Coaching can serve as a bridge to help schools become vibrant learning organizations in which teachers not only learn from each other, but get the support they need to use research that has been transformed into tools for practice.

This book is designed to explain the general tenets of Content-Focused Coaching and to provide specific examples of Content-Focused Coaching in action in elementary and middle school mathematics. The first chapter presents the general model and the underlying principles. Chapter Two, "Working with Teachers," provides practical advice for getting started and outlines the basic structure of coaching sessions. Next we present three case studies that illustrate Content-Focused Coaching in practice. The accompanying CDs contain video footage from both the coaching sessions and the lessons described in the case studies. They also contain full transcripts of the video segments and are designed to be used along with the book or independently as tools for study groups. The chapters titled, "The Principal" and "The District" situate the role of the coach or staff developer in the landscape of a school district and provide practical advice for negotiating that landscape. The final chapter highlights some strategies that can be used to transition teachers from teaching to coaching. It includes voices from the field—coaches speaking out about challenges, frustrations, and lessons learned as they valiantly strive to meet the needs of a changing and challenging profession.

The work described in this book is evolving. It has had a positive impact on our efforts to cultivate a professional learning community in Community School District 2 in New York City. Over a period of five years, 1997–2002, twenty coaches and sixty teacher leaders have been engaging in content-focused dialogues and working side-by-side with about 1,000 teachers and principals across the district. These efforts continue. We have a common curriculum and agreed-upon principles of learning, and we continue to collaboratively hone our teaching skills and deepen our content knowledge on a regular basis.

Through this book and the accompanying CDs, we offer our work as a catalyst for conversation among educators. We know that Content-

Focused Coaching can be one of many useful models of professional development in the quest to positively affect teaching and learning. We offer our experiences with it in the spirit of joining a national conversation on improving mathematics education.

Chapter One

What Is Content-Focused Coaching?

Fritz C. Staub, Lucy West, and
Donna DiPrima Bickel

The impact and effectiveness of traditional professional development seminars and workshops has increasingly been questioned by educators and researchers (Fullan 1995; Huberman 1995; Wilson & Berne 1999). Efforts to introduce new teaching strategies are more successful if in-class coaching is part of the training (Joyce & Showers 1995; Showers, Joyce & Bennett 1987). There is, however, no generally accepted coaching model: specific structures, scripts, and procedures vary greatly (see also, Anderson & Snyder 1993; Brand 1989; Costa & Garmston 1994; Schön 1987). For example, is the relationship between coach and teacher supervisory or collegial? Does the coach help the teacher understand underlying theory or train the teacher in specific skills and methods?

Coaching is especially popular in business (Thomas 1995; Whitmore 1992), where the coach's primary role is to facilitate reflection and growth. Identifying specific problems is the client's task, not to be taken over by the coach. Coaches frequently know very little about the client's business. This kind of coaching is especially appropriate with regard to personal problems and personal growth.

Coaching in the teaching profession, which is designed to scale up teaching expertise, must be much more specific. Coaches themselves need to be excellent teachers in the same discipline as the teacher being coached, able to provide situation-specific assistance adapted to that teacher. Content-Focused Coaching is a professional development model designed to promote student learning and achievement by

1

having a coach and a teacher work jointly in specific settings, guided by conceptual tools (Staub, West & Miller 1998; Staub 1999; Staub 2001). Coach and teacher collaboratively plan, enact, and reflect on specific lessons, acting as resources for each other. In Content-Focused Coaching, theory-based conceptual tools assist coaches and teachers in deciding what to focus on in coaching conversations and how to guide such conversations. A framework for lesson design and analysis (Figure 1–1), a set of principles of learning (Figure 1–2 and Appendix 1), and a set of core issues in mathematics lesson design (Figures 1–3 and 1–4) help coaches guide teachers' thinking in relation to the highly complex tasks of lesson design and classroom teaching, and about the issues surrounding student learning. In addition, goals and coaching moves provide concepts for reflecting on, guiding and developing coaching conversations.

Content-Focused Coaching is related to apprenticeship, in which an apprentice is observed while carrying out a task and the master craftsman offers hints, provides support, gives feedback, models, gives reminders, and poses new tasks aimed at bettering performance (Collins, Brown & Newman 1989). Such assistance may be highly idiosyncratic. Content-Focused Coaching is distinguished from traditional apprenticeship in that the guidance is informed by a conceptual framework that is supported by specific tools. In addition, coaches still view themselves as learners, continuing to refine their teaching, learning, and coaching as a result of the lessons they coach and the conversation they cultivate.

Even knowledgeable master teachers are not always successful when working with adults, so coaches must have excellent social skills and be able to communicate effectively. Coaching a teacher in the classroom necessitates communication and coordination among coach, teacher, and students.

Content-Focused Coaching centers on students' learning in the lessons but is also about teachers' learning from the process. In the short term, teachers refine how they teach particular lessons to specific groups of students. In the long term, they develop professional habits of mind and general teaching expertise. Expert teachers know both their subject and the best pedagogical practices by which to bring the subject to their students. Content-Focused Coaching zeroes in on the daily tasks of planning, teaching, and reflecting on lessons by suggesting a framework and tools for addressing standards, curriculum, principles of learning, and lesson design and assessment. It does *not* prescribe particular methods or techniques of teaching.

To be most effective, Content-Focused Coaching has to be seen in relation to and coordinated with other elements of professional development. The challenge in onsite coaching is to help teachers design and implement successful lessons and to engage with and reflect on the issues that are relevant to student learning. Prerequisites include establishing trusting working relationships among principal, coach, and teachers and building organizational structures within schools so that coaching can take place.

Goals and Features

Content-Focused Coaching is not a quick fix for bad teachers. Instead, it provides structures for ongoing professional development that

- Helps teachers design and implement lessons from which students will learn.
- Is content specific. Teachers' plans, strategies, and methods are discussed in terms of students learning a particular subject.
- Is based on a set of core issues of learning and teaching.
- Fosters professional habits of mind.
- Enriches and refines teachers' pedagogical content knowledge.
- Encourages teachers to communicate with each other about issues of teaching and learning in a focused and professional manner.

The Setting

Content-Focused Coaching takes place in schools. The teacher and coach have a prelesson conference; observe, teach, or coteach the lesson; and have a postlesson conference. The coach and the teacher are jointly accountable for initiating and assisting effective student learning. This very important feature ensures that the coach is intimately involved in all aspects of the lesson. Depending on a particular teacher's needs and background, a coach's active involvement may vary considerably. When pre- and postlesson conferences are held and how long they last also varies considerably and depends on district and school policy. (These issues are dealt with more specifically in the chapters on working with the teacher, the principal, and the district.)

The Prelesson Conference

At the prelesson conference, the teacher explains the goals for the lesson and how he or she plans to teach it. The coach becomes acquainted with the teacher's thinking, beliefs, and knowledge. They talk about how the lesson will foster student learning and how curriculum materials can be a starting point for customizing lessons to fit particular students. Teacher and coach collaboratively design or redesign a particular lesson or aspects of a lesson. Developing a shared view of the understanding, strategies, concepts, and skills that students are working toward, together with agreeing on a lesson design, makes it possible to have postlesson discussions focused on student learning. Establishing clear, explicit learning goals related to specific content also increases the likelihood that the lessons will revolve around important mathematical ideas and that the coach and teacher will work together effectively during the lesson.

The Lesson

A coach's role during a lesson can vary considerably. She or he may enter different kinds of collaborations with the teacher and take on the responsibility for conducting different parts of the lesson. A coach's involvement may increase from *observing* only, to *coteaching* the lesson, to *modeling* the lesson while the teacher observes. Because lesson plans are shared or coconstructed during the preconference, the coach and the teacher are to some extent jointly responsible even for lessons that are taught solely by the teacher. Teacher and coach negotiate how they will collaborate during a specific lesson based on the teacher's needs (stated by teacher and perceived by coach) and on what will make the lesson one in which students learn.

Modeling is especially appropriate when a coach wants to demonstrate specific teaching strategies or methods (such as ways of leading accountable talk in the classroom). The goal of modeling is for the teacher to build an understanding of new teaching moves. Modeling often is the start of a longer process during which the teacher learns to use the new strategies.

Even during lessons that are taught primarily by the classroom teacher, the coach's role is collaborative. This may mean, for example, that the coach intervenes during the lesson—but only in a particular way. The coach negotiates in advance whether the teacher is comfortable with this kind of intervention. The intervention is never directed toward something the teacher may have done inadequately; rather, the coach addresses students' understanding and learning, perhaps by asking a question related to a student's crucial idea or particular misconception. Coaches and teachers are jointly accountable for initiating and assisting effective student learning. The coach is a partner with the teacher in working toward the shared goal of student learning, not a critic of the teacher's practice. Over time, the coach will decrease and eventually phase out modeling and situation-specific interventions.

The Postlesson Conference

After the lesson, the teacher and the coach talk about how the lesson went. How successfully was the lesson plan implemented? What problems arose? More important, did the students learn what they were supposed to? This joint evaluation often includes looking at student work. If necessary, the conversation also addresses the lesson's appropriateness to the goals set—and even the appropriateness of the goals themselves. Postlesson conferences often segue into a prelesson conference for the next lesson.

What Should Coaching Conversations Focus On?

Different issues emerge during coaching conversations. In the preconference, teacher and coach mostly deliberate goals and lesson plans. During the lesson, they participate in classroom talk and perhaps have a brief private exchange about a whole-class teaching move or how to help individual students. During the postconference, student learning and challenges met during the lesson come to the fore. Whatever the setting, there are an infinite number of potential issues that can be addressed.

A Framework for Lesson Design

Teaching is a very complex activity (Bromme 1992; Stigler & Hiebert 1999; Leinhardt 1993). It can be looked at from many perspectives and discussed at different levels of abstraction, depending on one's knowledge, theories, and beliefs. The conceptual frame presented here reflects a profound change in the definition of teaching—from teaching as *mechanically implementing* curriculum to teaching as *mindfully making use of* curriculum. Teaching requires sophisticated reasoning in choosing and prioritizing lesson goals and designing lessons that enable a given group of students to reach given standards. At the core of this kind of reasoning are two basic questions:

1. *What is the curricular content to be learned by the students?* This question is often answered by naming curricular themes, tasks, or activities, or by describing instructional strategies. Although all of these relate in various ways to what students are to learn in a particular lesson, they do not fully capture the subject matter to be learned. Goals for what students are to learn at a given grade level are delineated in district, state, or national standards. In order to state the learning in a lesson specifically, teachers must

know—thoroughly—the particular content and how it relates to the standards.

2. *How is this content to be taught?* What are the teacher's underlying teaching methods and strategies? The execution of a lesson can be described and discussed in terms of specific practices and general teaching methods, such as inquiry-based learning, using worksheets, and cooperative groupings. The teacher's repertoire of methods and strategies determines the number of potential teaching moves he or she has to choose from.

Lesson design takes place at the intersection of *what* and *how*. What is the relationship between curriculum and teachers' work in the classroom? In the United States, curriculum is most often thought of as an "organizational framework, a 'curriculum-as-manual,' containing the templates for coverage and methods that are seen as guiding, directing, or controlling a school's, or a school system's, day-by-day classroom work" (Westbury 2000, 17). In other words, these manuals set forth *what* to teach and *how* to teach it. For a time, it was even hoped that a "technology of teaching" would lead to fully specified curricula that would guarantee effective teaching no matter who the teacher happened to be. The aim of constructing "teacher-proof" curricula, however, has turned out to be out of reach and based on a naïve conception of what effective teaching involves. Even when curriculum materials specify lessons in some detail, a competent teacher still needs

Figure 1–1
Framework for Lesson Design and Analysis
(adapted from Staub 1999, 2001)

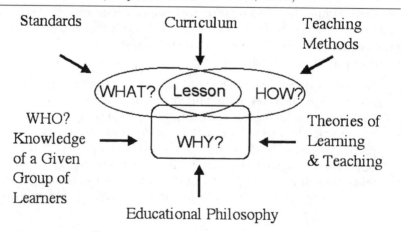

to adapt a given lesson to the context of the particular classroom and to the individual characteristics, needs, and backgrounds of the learners in it.

When teachers are encouraged to be thoughtful professionals who do more than follow their intuition based on experience and traditions, then they deliberate about and debate *why* they choose particular content or methods. There are therefore two more basic questions at the core of teachers' professional reasoning:

3. *Why is this specific content to be taught?*

4. *Why will it be taught in this particular way?*

In addressing these basic questions, teachers choose the subject matter, transform it into lesson content, and design lessons that help students reach standards. We don't mean that these basic questions need to be posed literally in this abstract form. The general *what, how,* and *why* questions are guiding heuristics for thoughtful teaching. Taking up these questions in connection with each other leads to new learning and new insights about how particular content can be taught effectively to the students of a given classroom or why a specific method is especially suited to a particular learning goal. In addressing these questions, coach and teacher also draw on available research about which strategies and methods work effectively for specific purposes. Posing the generic questions alone, however, doesn't get the work done. For teachers to recall or construct appropriate answers, they must be knowledgeable about content, standards, teaching methods, curricula, assessment, the theory and psychology of learning and teaching, and educational philosophy.

When *why* questions cannot be answered by referring to an existing standard, a curriculum, or regularly practiced teaching methods, teachers need to reason deliberately about their design choices. Such deliberation, however, presupposes criteria and theories. By what criteria do we decide on the particular content and a specific design for a lesson? Teachers have a lot of leeway in how they choose to help their students achieve a given standard. How we deliberate about *why* a particular method is useful for teaching specific content to a given group of students depends on our beliefs and theories about learning and teaching, our knowledge about research on effective practices and about the particular learners to be taught, and on our educational philosophy. What teachers believe about the learning and teaching of a specific subject matters not only to how they behave in the classroom but also to student achievement (Staub & Stern 2002). While districts can mandate particular instructional programs and approaches, a change in teaching practice will only be sustained over time if it is supported by coherent underlying beliefs.

Only part of the knowledge that is relevant to lesson design can be acquired through experience and experimentation. It is primarily through interaction with knowledgeable others, texts, and tools that teachers revise their beliefs and develop habits of mind and knowledge relevant to effective lesson design.

An Orientation Toward the Content of Learning and Teaching

During much of the twentieth century, the dominance of behaviorist and associationist theories of learning meant that content and pedagogy were often dealt with separately. European theories of education and teaching rooted in philosophy (Klafki 1963) and based on a cognitive view of learning and teaching (Aebli 1951, 1983) argued against this separation between teaching methods and content. Klafki's and Aebli's general theories of teaching (known as *Didaktik*) share an orientation toward the content of learning and teaching. Effective and responsible teaching requires educators to thoroughly think through the meaning and the structure of the content to be taught. Clarifying the underlying structure has primacy over questions about how to teach a particular content. When designing lessons, clarifying the *what* usually precedes specifying the *how*. To grasp the design of a given lesson unit from curriculum manuals, teachers must clearly understand the intended *what*, as well as *why* an already given *how*, supports learners in reaching the goals. Such reasoning may lead teachers to modify the *how* or even to change the lesson's goals. Teachers' anticipation of and planning for specific teaching–learning processes are intimately related to the content. The teaching of subject matter has to be understood in relation to the particular content and the learners being taught.

Cognitive psychology has demonstrated the important role of knowledge in reasoning, thinking, and learning (Aebli 1981; Resnick 1987). Learning is an active process of interpretation and inference based on what people already know. Resnick and Hall (1998) refer to the core of this theory of learning as *knowledge-based constructivism*. There is no thinking without content, and without thinking there is no acquisition of new knowledge. There is no direct transmission of knowledge. For the cognitive-constructivist, learning is an active process through which learners construct new knowledge on the basis of the cognitive structures already available. The teachers' role is to initiate learning and to prompt and assist particular learners as they construct rigorous, specific knowledge. Coaching conversations that are meant to help teachers develop practical ways to initiate and guide student learning thus need to be very content specific.

Knowing what methods and teaching strategies are useful for helping students learn a specific content and how to adapt these methods and strategies to particular learners is the pivotal ingredient in teaching expertise. Shulman (1987) calls this kind of knowledge *pedagogical content knowledge*, "the blending of content and pedagogy into an understanding of how particular topics, problems, or issues are organized, represented, and adapted to the diverse interests and abilities of learners, and presented for instruction" (8). Not all of this knowledge is explicit. Some of it is based on experience alone and remains implicit. It is the coach's role to focus on and make explicit those aspects that are highly relevant in a given situation.

A knowledgeable other (the coach or the teacher, in Content-Focused Coaching) can introduce any knowledge related to the *what, how,* and *why* of a specific teaching situation. Elements brought up by a coach or through discussion or her or his own teaching may lead to teaching situations that are different from what the teacher would have arrived at alone. Coaching conversations that address and relate the *what, how,* and *why* of lessons can foster learning that goes beyond situation-specific assistance and therefore builds explicit pedagogical content knowledge.

Core Issues in Lesson Design

A set of research-based principles of learning proposed by Lauren Resnick (Resnick 1995a, 1995b) and further developed by the Institute for Learning (Resnick & Hall 2001) succinctly captures pivotal theories of learning and teaching that are believed to be relevant for an educational system designed to enable all students to achieve a high level of performance. Figure 1–2 depicts three of these principles (see Appendix 1 for the list of all nine principles).

For these principles of learning to be of practical use in lesson design, they need to be related to the kind of reasoning teachers use daily in the classroom. Therefore, the coach participates on the job, helping the teacher deliberately plan and teach lessons that produce student learning. The principles of learning are general and abstract. In order for coaching conversations to reach a content-specific level when designing and reflecting on lessons, Content-Focused Coaching makes use of an additional kind of tool, the Guide to Core Issues in Mathematics Lesson Design (see Figure 1–3). The questions in this guide prompt the coach and teacher to address issues at the heart of instruction in content-specific ways (Staub, West, Miller 1998; Staub 1999).

The idea for such a tool is based on a set of questions, developed by Klafki (1958, 1995), that is meant to ensure that teachers' long-term

Figure 1–2
Three of the Institute for Learning's Nine Principles of Learning
(Resnick & Hall 2001)

Clear Expectations

If we expect all students to achieve at high levels, then we need to define explicitly what we expect students to learn. These expectations need to be communicated clearly in ways that get them "into the heads" of school professionals, parents, the community, and, above all, the students. Descriptive criteria and models of work that meet standards should be publicly displayed, and students should refer to these displays to help them analyze and discuss their work. With visible accomplishment targets to aim toward at each stage of learning, students can participate in evaluating their own work and setting goals for their own effort.

Academic Rigor in a Thinking Curriculum

Thinking and problem solving will be the "new basics" of the twenty-first century. But the common idea that we can teach thinking without a solid foundation of knowledge must be abandoned. So must the idea that we can teach knowledge without engaging students in thinking. Knowledge and thinking are intimately joined. This implies a curriculum organized around major concepts that students are expected to know deeply. Teaching must engage students in active reasoning about these concepts. In every subject, at every grade level, instruction and learning must include commitment to a knowledge core, high thinking demand, and active use of knowledge.

Accountable Talk[SM]

Talking with others about ideas and work is fundamental to learning. But not all talk sustains learning. For classroom talk to promote learning it must be accountable—to the learning community, to accurate and appropriate knowledge, and to rigorous thinking. Accountable talk seriously responds to and further develops what others in the group have said. It puts forth and demands knowledge that is accurate and relevant to the issue under discussion. Accountable talk uses evidence appropriate to the discipline (e.g., proofs in mathematics, data from investigations in science, textual details in literature, documentary sources in history) and follows established norms of good reasoning. Teachers should intentionally create the norms and skills of accountable talk in their classrooms.

---

curricular and lesson planning is accountable to the underlying structures of the discipline, takes into account the learners' prior experience and knowledge that are relevant to the learning goal at hand, and anticipates future contexts in which the knowledge to be learned may lead to useful applications. The selection of the kind of theoretical perspectives taken up with the questions in the Guide to Core Issues in

Figure 1–3
Guide to Core Issues in Mathematics Lesson Design

What are the goals and the overall plan of the lesson?

- What is your plan?
- Where in your plan would you like some assistance?

(Based on the teacher's response, the coach focuses on one or more of the following ideas.)

What is the mathematics in this lesson? (i.e., make the lesson goals explicit)

- What is the specific mathematics goal of this lesson?
- What are the mathematics concepts?
- Are there specific strategies being developed? Explain.
- What skills (applications, practice) are being taught in this lesson?
- What tools are needed (e.g., calculators, rulers, protractors, pattern blocks, cubes)?

Where does this lesson fall in this unit and why? (i.e., clarify the relationship between the lesson, the curriculum, and the standards)

- Do any of these concepts and/or skills get addressed at other points in the unit?
- Which goal is your priority for this lesson?
- What does this lesson have to do with the concept you have identified as your primary goal?
- Which standards does this particular lesson address?

What are students' prior knowledge and difficulties?

- What relevant concepts have already been explored with this class?
- What strategies does this lesson build on?
- What relevant contexts (money, for example) could you draw on in relation to this concept?
- What can you identify or predict students may find difficult or confusing or have misconceptions about?
- What ideas might students begin to express and what language might they use?

How does the lesson help students reach the goals? (i.e., think through the implementation of the lesson)

- What grouping structure will you use and why?
- What opening question do you have in mind?
- How do you plan to present the tasks or problems?
- What model, manipulative, or visual will you use?
- What activities will move students toward the stated goals?

(continued)

Figure 1–3

(continued)

- In what ways will students make their mathematical thinking and understanding public?
- What will the students say or do that will demonstrate their learning?
- How will you ensure that students are talking with and listening to one another about important mathematics in an atmosphere of mutual respect?
- How will you ensure that the ideas being grappled with will be highlighted and clarified?
- How do you plan to assist those students who you predict will have difficulties?
- What extensions or challenges will you provide for students who are ready for them?
- How much time do you predict will be needed for each part of the lesson?

Mathematics Lesson Design, in addition to other sources, has been influenced by Aebli's general theory of teaching (Aebli 1983), which is grounded in cognitive psychology. Aebli's theory asks teachers to understand and thoroughly analyze the content to be taught and to think through and anticipate learning processes in content-specific terms. Teachers need to take into account that knowledge to be acquired is constructed using students' prior knowledge.

The coach should not use the questions in Figure 1–3 verbatim. The particular issues to be addressed and the wording of the questions used to address them need to be adapted based on the coach's knowledge of and relationship with the teacher. The questions are intended to prompt a shared understanding of the lesson's learning goals and a coordinated plan for and understanding of how students can be helped to achieve those goals.

Clarifying lesson goals is pivotal. For teachers to communicate Clear Expectations, they must be clear about the standards of achievement and specific goals of learning toward which their students are to work. Arriving at a clear understanding of the particular content-related goals of a lesson is also necessary to foster Accountable Talk[SM] and Academic Rigor in a Thinking Curriculum. Initiating and orchestrating talk that is truly accountable to accurate and appropriate knowledge and rigorous thinking requires the teacher to deeply know and have thought through the content of the discipline and to have clarified the learning goals. Teachers' explanations are also of great importance. The

Figure 1–4
Abbreviated List of Core Issues in
Mathematics Lesson Design

- Lesson goals.
- Lesson plan and design.
- Students' relevant prior knowledge.
- Relationship between the nature of the task and the activity on one hand and the lesson goals on the other hand.
- Strategies for students to make public their thinking and understanding.
- Evidence of students' understanding and learning.
- Students' difficulties, confusions, and misconceptions.
- Ways to encourage collaboration in an atmosphere of mutual respect.
- Strategies to foster relevant student discussion.

nature of classroom discourse contributes to or hinders students' socialization as intelligent and responsible members of their culture (Resnick and Nelson-LeGall 1997). In order to make reasoned decisions about appropriate learning goals and to fine-tune individualized student learning, teachers need to know about their students' prior knowledge as well as their difficulties and misconceptions. In order to assess student learning, teachers need to be clear about the evidence of successful learning and to think about how a lesson design will initiate and allow students to make public their thinking and knowing.

While a knowledge of all the Core Issues in Mathematics Lesson Design can be helpful to teachers and coaches, when first working with the Core Issues, it is impossible to focus consciously on all of them at once. Teachers and coaches are thus encouraged to concentrate on a few at a time. (An abbreviated version of the core issues is shown in Figure 1–4.) It is also important to understand that the core issues are *scaffolds:* prompts to get teachers to think through important aspects of learning and teaching. Scaffolds are by definition temporary. Once a new structure has been built, the scaffold can be removed. After coaches and teachers have worked with the Core Issues for some time, the related reasoning will ideally become second nature.

One way for coaches to learn to work with the Core Issues is to write and use their own summaries of the list shown in Figure 1–3. From time to time, however, it is helpful to go back to the original version and identify which issues they concentrate on in coaching conversations, then to make a conscious effort to incorporate the ones they tend to ignore.

Guiding and Developing Coaching Conversations

How does a coach know what to focus on in coaching conversations? In Content-Focused Coaching, two main goals guide the work of coaches. Although at times they may compete for priority, both must be kept at the fore and in balance. The two goals are

1. *Fostering student learning* in the coached lessons. The coach must help teachers, in practical ways, design and implement lessons that are conducive to student learning. The coach and teacher are jointly accountable for student learning.

2. *Supporting the professional development of teachers.* Coaching must help teachers develop habits of mind in lesson design, learn to reflect on their teaching, and enrich and refine their pedagogical content knowledge. It must also help them become better at communicating with each other about issues of teaching and learning in a focused and professional manner.

Settings that do not hold coaches jointly accountable for student learning and ask only that coaches give feedback on lessons already taught do of course result in interesting observations and suggestions; however, their practical impact on teachers' future actions is uncertain and remains untested. Content-Focused Coaching builds on the assumption that in order to best support teachers' professional development on the job, coaches and teachers need to be partners doing their very best to foster student learning in the coached lessons. The on-the-job setting is most likely to engage teachers and coaches in the complex work of designing and implementing lessons that are conducive to student learning. The focus on student learning thus becomes a guiding criterion for deciding which aspects of teaching need to be assisted.

Coaches assist the teachers they coach by way of *coaching moves.* A *move* is "any action that is accomplished with the intention of bringing about a state of affairs that directly or indirectly will (probably) lead to a desired global goal" (van Dijk & Kintsch 1983, 66). For example, flying from New York to Zurich may include the "moves" of taking a cab to the airport and boarding the plane. Incidental actions, such as reading a paper while riding to the airport, are not moves, because they are not functional in bringing about the desired final goal. In Content-Focused Coaching, all actions that a coach undertakes to work toward any of the two global goals of fostering student learning and developing teacher expertise are coaching moves. They may include observing a lesson, giving feedback, teaching a lesson, coteaching a lesson, intervening in classroom talk, suggesting lesson designs, assessing student learning, presenting a new teaching method, or explaining content, to name a few.

In particular, a coach may help a teacher by raising questions, making suggestions, and refining the teacher's plans with respect to what to teach and how to teach it. Coaches get teachers started and support them in making lesson goals explicit. Coaches also facilitate thinking through the design of the lesson in a content-focused way from theory-based points of view that are pivotal for student learning. Coaches not only help teachers deliver successful lessons, they also create opportunities for teachers to refine and develop their teaching expertise. Coaches may therefore also inject explanations relative to any of the knowledge areas depicted in the Framework for Lesson Design and Analysis (Figure 1–1). Coaches may even argue for certain designs. When a teacher's and a coach's views differ, the ultimate decision remains with the teacher. The teacher and coach can, in the postconference, discuss the extent to which the course of action chosen produced the desired outcome.

The most important power of coaching is the potential for highly interactive and collaborative processes, which allow the coach to fine-tune the help being offered to the individual and situation-specific needs of the teacher being coached. Such highly customized assistance, however, is only possible if coaches respect and take into account teachers' knowledge and underlying beliefs about learning and teaching by encouraging them to share and discuss their own ideas, suggestions, and reflections. Coaches also need to check their own understanding by paraphrasing and summarizing what the teacher has said. The pivotal aspects of coaching are accomplished through two basic kinds of coaching moves:

1. *Moves that invite teacher contributions.* Statements or questions by the coach that initiate and invite the teacher to verbalize perceptions, thoughts, plans, deliberations, and arguments.

2. *Moves that provide direct assistance with lesson design.* Statements by the coach that provide guidance and explanations for specific designs and ways of implementing a lesson.

Moves that invite teacher contributions can be very general: "So, tell me about this lesson." They can also be more specific, depending on the coach's knowledge of lesson design in general and understanding of the teacher's specific lesson plan:

Coach: Do you anticipate any confusion between the story and what you're trying to get them to do?

Teacher: I hope it will be clear. We've been talking about counting books and this is more of a counting book. However when we did counting books before, they had lots of different pieces of paper, and they knew they were drawing one and then two and then three. . . .

Variations of core issues may be used to stimulate teachers to think through and verbalize important aspects of a lesson. For example, the coach may ask, "How can we find out how students actually understand the task?" Such an invitation does not directly suggest how the lesson should look. In raising questions related to core issues, however, coach and teacher begin to communicate and deliberate about the design issues that are relevant to student learning and may need to coconstruct new or refined lesson designs.

Moves that provide direct assistance offer specific suggestions (and to some extent arguments) for lesson design in a particular teaching situation. For example:

Coach: Now I'm going to jump back here [pointing to the counting book]. I'm worried about using this book with those kids who may not understand the problem.

Teacher: Yeah.

Coach: So, if you are going to read this book, I think it's going to take you off your task. Even though it has the same title, the mathematics is different. Unless you wanted to make up a story about fruit salad that's more like this problem.

Teacher: Yeah, I think that would be better. Maybe I could say, "We've just had Thanksgiving, and there was a nice fruit salad for dessert, and there were only two kinds of fruit. . . ."

Moves to provide direct assistance need to be based on the coach's knowledge of the teacher's plans and understanding of the lesson. They don't need to specify a lesson design in full. They can also lead to genuine coconstructions by the coach and the teacher.

In order to support professional development, coaches need to keep a balance between invitational moves and moves of direct assistance. Guided only by the goal of fostering student learning, a coach may do too much of the work on lesson design and teaching, for too long, without creating enough opportunities for genuine collaboration with the teacher. On the other hand, it is not enough for coaches to limit themselves to eliciting teacher reflection with general questions and offer no direct assistance in designing the lesson. Based on their professional knowledge, coaches need to provide substantive contributions that will have an impact on the quality of the coached lessons and thus create opportunities for teachers to learn from practice. Some novice coaches tend to concentrate exclusively on being active listeners without providing substantive input that helps to design or analyze the teaching situation. Others deliver long prescriptive monologues without allowing the teacher to participate in a genuine dialogue. Naturally, given different levels of teaching expertise and different areas of learning, the balance between invitational moves and direct assistance will shift. While at times it may be useful for coaches to take on a lot of the design and teaching work, the long-term goal must be to phase out direct assistance.

In contrast to collegial coaching, Content-Focused Coaching expects coaches to have more teaching expertise than the teachers being coached do. Ideally, coaches should have hands-on knowledge in the discipline and be very familiar with official standards, teaching materials, teaching methods, students at the corresponding grade levels, and theories of learning and teaching. (There are, of course, many exceptions to this ideal.) Because of their respective levels of professional knowledge, the interaction between teacher and coach will not be symmetrical.

Despite these differences, however, certain conditions and strategies foster professional collegiality between coach and teacher. First, the coach does not have the power to formally evaluate the teacher (the principal usually does). Second, based on the coach's accountability for student learning during the coached lessons, the coach's main focus is on what the teacher can do to assist the students' content-specific learning, not on evaluating how well the teacher uses specific teaching methods. Furthermore, coaches understand (or learn to understand) themselves as learners. They acknowledge that each new lesson design and each enactment of a lesson is to a certain extent an inherently uncertain creative act from which something can be learned. A stance of genuine curiosity and collaboration can be made manifest by wording suggestions tentatively: "I wonder if doing such-and-so would . . ." Productive collaboration that successfully fosters student learning will strengthen a trusting relationship between teacher and coach.

Chapter Two

Working with Teachers

Coaches who have been classroom teachers themselves understand the complexity of teaching and its centrality to helping all students achieve high levels of learning. Professional development adds another layer of complexity because it focuses on the teacher's learning in order to improve student learning. The coach needs to not only understand what is involved in teaching children, but also have the skill set to work with adults as they navigate the change process and build their own content and pedagogical knowledge. Coaches need to become astute at diagnosing the stated and unstated needs of the teachers they work with, mapping the relationships in a school, getting the pulse of the school culture, and developing a repertoire of strategies that allow for differentiated staff development. This is analogous to learning to meet the needs of a range of students in a math class.

In-classroom coaching is a piece of the puzzle of systemic change and coaches need to situate their work with individual teachers into the large picture. Keeping the larger picture in mind can, in turn, provide focus for work with individual teachers. For example, if the larger school community is focused on effective strategies for developing computational proficiency among students, the coaching work with individual teachers should reflect this goal. Each teacher is an interdependent facet of a loosely connected complex system. The coaching with each teacher will have a ripple effect on the professional community at the school. By the same token, if teachers are also attending workshops on developing effective instructional strategies for teaching computation and on deepening their own understanding of number operations, it will complement the coaching. The object is to create a learning community at the school level that is aligned with the work on the district level. In practical terms this means focusing on building relationships with and among teachers by helping them build the skill set needed for effective instruction, and helping them create self-sustaining networks that will result in ongoing improvement. Thinking about the larger picture and situating the individual within it helps the staff developer prioritize the scope of the work.

Diagnosing Teachers' Needs

It is essential to consider what teachers know and can do and what they need to learn and be able to do. The gap between the two is the scope of the coaching work. "Where do I begin?" is a lament of many a novice coach. While there is no recipe, we will consider the following areas:

- content knowledge and disposition toward mathematics
- pedagogical knowledge and underlying beliefs about learning
- pedagogical content knowledge
- diagnosing children's thinking and assessing prior knowledge
- habits of planning and engagement with curriculum materials.

While all of these are interwoven and get worked on simultaneously, usually one of them is more glaringly a need or a strength than the others are. Considering the teacher in relation to these five areas helps the coach get an overview of the scope of the coaching work that's to be done.

Content Knowledge and Disposition Toward Mathematics

Content knowledge involves a deep and flexible knowledge of the mathematics that is to be taught. This includes an understanding of the network of concepts that relate to the specific concept to be taught and of how that network is connected to the mathematics in the year-long curriculum as well as to the curricula of the previous and following years.

Sometimes it is evident early on that a teacher is "math phobic" and lacks confidence in her or his content knowledge. A teacher's attitude toward mathematics will, of course, impact her or his effectiveness in teaching mathematics. Clearly, you cannot teach what you do not know. Sometimes, however, teachers are reticent to express a dislike of the subject or insecurity about their content knowledge; they act as if they know, and are defensive about their practice. Teachers, like most people, fear making mistakes and exposing what they don't know. Other teachers have inflated confidence in their knowledge of mathematics. As a result, coaches often find themselves trying to teach content in the planning session, doing the mathematics with teachers as they prepare to teach their lessons. Coaches are often classroom teachers who are relearning mathematics themselves, and who continue to do so in their coaching role. This can become an opportunity for coach and teacher to explore mathematics together. Coaches will also have to work with colleagues who know more mathematics than they do. In this way, teachers and coaches are truly collaborative learners. We are not suggesting that mathematics can be effectively taught during coaching sessions. A teacher who needs to learn more mathematics in order to teach the curriculum will have to attend workshops or classes designed to increase content knowledge. For many of us, giving a specific and meaningful answer to "what is the mathematics in this lesson," is often a challenge. The commitment should be to continue learning mathematics content.

Pedagogical Knowledge and Underlying Beliefs About Learning

Pedagogy includes developing and maintaining a classroom environment that is conducive to learning, management structures that provide opportunities for self-management of learning and behavior, and instructional strategies and techniques that serve the needs of a range of learners. Evidence of learning is the bottom line. Coaches must be very careful to give teachers leeway in finding a teaching style that suits them and results in rich, deep, flexible learning. A coach's dogmatic insistence on a particular pedagogical stance usually leads to the teacher's digging in of the heels rather than to a willingness to reconsider beliefs.

Coaches need to be very aware of their own beliefs about learning and biases about pedagogy. To engage teachers in genuine dialogue about their underlying beliefs about learning and teaching, coaches must respectfully understand the teachers' beliefs, whatever they may be. It is a good idea to avoid ideological entrenchment and to look for common ground that can provide openings for constructive collaboration. Teachers become engaged in collaboration and learning through working side by side and deliberating with a coach who demonstrates an open and curious mind and a constant willingness to learn from personal experience as well as from research.

The key is to keep evidence of student learning at the core. If a teacher is more authoritarian in management style and a coach is more democratic in approach, these differences will need to be noted and considered in relation to student learning. Reformers in mathematics education tend to be child-centered in their pedagogical approaches and to value teaching methods that are based on constructivist notions of learning. Some teachers embrace notions of teaching that are more directive, in which students are expected to employ only demonstrated procedures and strategies and to develop understanding through practice. These differing belief systems usually result in very different management styles and classroom cultures. Reformers want to develop "learning communities" in which students are required to think, listen, argue, and puzzle over mathematical ideas with their peers. The more traditional approach expects students to listen to teacher explanations and to work independently. The latter approach often results in behavior modification structures that are controlled by the teacher, such as stars for "good" work or behavior and visits to the time-out chair for "bad." The former requires that students regulate their own behavior and develop effective interpersonal skills. Teacher and students engage in conversations during which mutually agreed-upon rules and codes of behavior are made explicit.

If there are serious management issues in a classroom, it is very difficult to focus on the content: If students are not listening to each other or the teacher, if they call out and distract each other, and if the teacher resorts to yelling or punitive strategies, it is very difficult to have meaningful conversations about mathematics. If this is the case, coaching dialogues will revolve around developing a culture in which learning can take place. The coach needs to be able to articulate and model clear and specific methods and strategies for a teacher to try if progress is to be made. One way to approach this is to begin with an inquiry into the teacher's image of an ideal class. Can the teacher imagine what it would look like, feel like, and sound like if the class were working in the way he or she wanted? If the teacher can articulate that and make it explicit, he or she can then make explicit agreements with students about how they will function in class. Often the teacher's ideal is similar to the coach's, although their beliefs about creating the ideal may be different. If there is a common destination, the coach can assist the teacher in creating the ideal class.

Guiding all students to proficiency in mathematics involves being willing to become aware of one's biases and beliefs about who can learn and how learning takes place. Staff developers disagree about whether people must change their beliefs before they change their practice or whether a change in practice brings about a change in beliefs. In our experience, it is often a combination of new practices, new curricula, and a willingness to suspend belief and reflect on evidence of learning that assists people in the process.

Pedagogical Content Knowledge

Pedagogical content knowledge is the knowledge base that is specific to effective mathematics instruction, including curricula and knowing how to unpack big mathematical ideas into accessible concepts for students. It includes the selection of appropriate tasks and curriculum materials and the creation of visuals, mathematical models, and explanations that give all students entry into the conceptual domain that's under study.

For example, when teaching fractions, it is effective to use both an area model and a division context to help students develop a flexible understanding. In one of the cases presented in this book, the teacher uses Geoboards as an area model to explore halves, fourths, and eighths. In another case, the children share a given number of brownies among a given set of people, thereby working with fractions as division. Pedagogical content knowledge in this case lies in being aware that both of these contexts contribute to a robust understanding of fractions.

Teachers may know a great deal of mathematics but not know how to make it understandable to their students. They forget what it was like to not know, or they never had to struggle to grasp the concepts in the first place. It is difficult for people for whom mathematics came easy to understand the difficulties and confusions of those for whom it doesn't. Teachers who can't make their own knowledge understandable tend to lack pedagogical content knowledge.

Diagnosing Children's Thinking and Assessing Prior Knowledge

Elementary school teachers often take several courses in teaching reading, at least one of which involves diagnosing reading problems. This is not the case for mathematics. In many states, teachers are required to take only one class in mathematics education and rarely does this course revolve around diagnosing children's struggles with understanding mathematics. Beyond some very basic early number ideas, most teachers do not really know how to diagnose children's thinking about mathematics, and they are at a loss in determining the gaps in children's knowledge.

Coaching sessions should include making explicit what children are likely to do or say in relation to the activity under discussion and what aspects of the concept might cause confusion. During the lesson, the coach and teacher should focus on what children actually do and say in order to build their knowledge base. Coaching sessions should often include activities like looking at student work together and reflecting on student comments as ways of building the teacher's knowledge about how children learn mathematics. These activities can lead to intelligent experimentation with interventions that might help children move through the various stages of development.

Many staff developers and teacher leaders are learning how to listen to children and how to think about the trajectories of development, misconceptions, partial knowledge, and common confusion that children experience as they learn mathematics. This is an area in which teachers and coaches can work as collaborative partners. In District 2, staff developers take courses (such as Developing Mathematical Ideas [DMI] see, Schifter, Bastable & Russell 1999a, 1999b for course materials) that are designed to help teachers learn to listen to children as they try to articulate their ideas, then discuss the implications for teaching. The staff developers then share this work with teachers.

Habits of Planning and Engagement with Curriculum Materials

Lesson planning and long-term planning need lots of attention in the coaching process. Many teachers think that they need to work with curriculum materials as if they are scripts to be followed almost mindlessly. At the other extreme are teachers who think they need to create each lesson from scratch. There is a steep learning curve for most people in becoming familiar with new curriculum units and learning to use them effectively. A great deal of the staff developers' work in District 2 revolves around helping teachers consider new ways of thinking about the role of curriculum materials. It is rare for teachers to try out activities before they ask children to do them. Teachers often lament the lack of time to plan thoroughly, and they sometimes admit to being unsure of how to plan effective mathematics lessons. Here, the Guide to Core Issues in Mathematics Lesson Design (Figure 1–3) is helpful. When used as a map for lesson planning, this tool helps teachers and coaches internalize pivotal questions they might ask themselves when planning lessons.

Getting to Know the Teacher

The first conversation between coach and teacher is one of exploration. The long-term goal is that the coach and teacher will establish a professional partnership that results in all students learning at high levels. Getting to know one another's strengths and styles, professional dreams and goals, and philosophies and beliefs is part of the journey.

The purpose of the first conversation is to establish a mutual agreement to work together, to begin to define the parameters of that work, and to lay out a plan of action, or at least a framework, that feels comfortable and productive to both parties. As in all productive human relationships, it is important that the dialogue be open and that there be no hidden agenda.

There is no recipe for what should be discussed in the first coaching session. The immediate goal is to uncover the teacher's needs as quickly as possible and translate them into a course of action. To get the ball rolling, the coach informally interviews the teacher by asking questions like the ones that follow.

How long have you been teaching? New teachers generally have different issues than experienced teachers do. Management and routines, for example, may be plaguing the new teacher, while for a veteran teacher management may no longer be an issue. However, the management structures that a veteran teacher has employed to date may need to be modified if they do not allow for student discourse and active, collaborative, problem solving.

New teachers may or may not have taken classes in their preparatory programs that were in line with research-based best practice or standards-based pedagogy. Veteran teachers may have never experienced the kind of learning environment they are now being asked to create and manage. This may trigger resistance to the new methods, or a sense of inadequacy that plays out as defensiveness or denial of the need to change. On the other hand, a veteran teacher who is a lifelong learner may have signed up for every institute or workshop offered and be delighted to have a partner with whom to bounce off ideas and extend her or his repertoire. Experience level influences the focus of the work, but stereotyping based on experience level is not conducive to productive rapport. All teachers are unique individuals who have been influenced by their teaching experience in myriad ways.

Another factor to consider is the experience level of the teacher in relation to the experience level of the coach. Coaches tend to enjoy working with new teachers because they feel they have a lot to offer to novices. The confidence this gives them helps them to dive in. In most instances teachers new to the profession are eager for support and guidance. However, when a senior teacher works with a coach who is quite a bit younger and has less teaching experience, the coach often experiences doubt and fears that she or he will not have anything of value to offer. Coaches often worry that they do not have the right to offer advice to veteran teachers, or to colleagues in general. Content-Focused Coaching is a collaboration in which each person respects the knowledge base and perspectives of the other and learning is reciprocal. The coach is not expected to arrive on the scene with a completely planned lesson. The teacher's input is always part of the coaching dialogue. It is often helpful for both teacher and coach to put these issues on the table and speak honestly about what they are feeling in order to set a productive tone for the work. Explicitly acknowledging that they will learn from each other and that each brings some piece of the puzzle to the table not only reduces insecurity, it is also the disposition needed in any learning community.

What are your favorite subjects to teach? How often do you teach mathematics? If teachers do not mention mathematics among their favorite subjects, that is a clue that they may not enjoy mathematics or feel confident in their content knowledge. If this is the case, they may not be giving mathematics adequate instructional time. Inadequate instructional time turned out to be one of the main reasons for poor student performance in District 2. (The rule of thumb in the district is that five hours a week should be dedicated to mathematics instruction.) In some schools, the overall schedule adversely impacts a teacher's ability to devote the necessary amount of time to teaching mathematics. The teacher may, in fact, be frustrated by the shortage of time allowed for mathematics instruction. If it is a schoolwide issue, the staff developer will have to make it a long-term goal to get the principal to consider mathematics instructional time when creating the overall school schedule. In the meantime, the coaching and teaching work will have to proceed within the given parameters. This is a very common scenario and one that often requires a year or two to remedy.

What are your feelings toward mathematics? A teacher's disposition toward a subject is important to the effectiveness of his or her instruction (Ma 1999). If a teacher dislikes the subject, part of the coaching sessions may be spent in finding ways to get the teacher to engage as a learner in a new way and to experience success in doing so.

What's your math history? If the previous question seems too direct or doesn't yield a useful response, asking the teacher to share an anecdote from their personal mathematics history may help. "I remember my second-grade teacher embarrassing me when I couldn't recite my facts fast enough" sheds a different light than "I always did well in math." Emotions play a big role in change, and applying emotional intelligence is a core coaching skill. It is important to not make assumptions based on statements like the ones above, but to instead use such statements as springboards for further probing.

Tell me about your students. It is important to pay close attention to the things a teacher says about her or his students, because further probing will likely reveal a lot about the teacher's beliefs about teaching and learning. For example, consider the statement "I love these kids, but they come from such dysfunctional homes." Is there an implication that pushing these students would be in vain because they will never have the kind of preconditions necessary to be successful learners? Or is there an implication that we may need to be really creative in helping children whose home lives are challenging develop the skills to learn at high standards? Either is plausible. The former belief implies an ability-based view of learning and the latter implies that the teacher sees it as her job to find a way to reach every student. Teachers' beliefs about students will impact student self-efficacy, which plays a pivotal role in success.

Are there colleagues you enjoy working with? What kinds of work-related things do you do together? These questions are aimed at mapping the relationships in the school, determining the level of collegiality, and helping you plan your schedule. You will want to build on existing relationships. In a case where two of four fifth-grade teachers on staff are already collaborating, ask the principal to give them a joint preparation period and combine their preconference to serve both. Because the goal is to build capacity, it is important to be on the lookout for ways to increase the number of teachers who can be served without decreasing the quality of service. If a cadre of teachers who are willing to start the journey can be identified, in no time at all the staff developer will have friendly allies who will assist and advise as she or he learns to navigate the culture of the school. They are likely to talk to their colleagues about the successes they are enjoying, which in turn will inspire others to get involved.

At the same time, it is important not to alienate those who may not be ready to plunge in. Eventually, if a school is going to have a coherent, effective, empowering mathematics program, all teachers will need to sign on. It will become more difficult to develop a professional learning community that serves all teachers on the staff if those who are eager to start are seen as elitists and those who are more reluctant to sign on are alienated. Suffice it to say that coaches must do their best to maintain the fine balance between inviting people into the fold and giving people the time and space they may need to come aboard voluntarily.

What are your goals as a learner? What are you curious about in relation to teaching and learning? Questions like these imply that learning is part of the professional domain and is ongoing. They also begin to move the conversation to the specifics of the work. Here, too, listening carefully to a teacher's response can be revealing. A teacher who has some clear and specific goals is likely to be a self-motivated learner. If the motivation for learning is intrinsic, a teacher will be committed to the work that is codefined in coaching sessions. A teacher who can't think of any areas she or he would like to know more about may not be habitually self-reflective about her or his practice; that teacher's locus of motivation might be external. People who are externally motivated will often comply with the changes being demanded of them, but will not necessarily internalize the underlying principles. Often they implement the more superficial aspects of the improvement program and their essential practice remains unchanged. For example, they might change the room arrangement from desks in rows to desks in clusters of four, but give assignments that almost all call for independent work. If this is the case, the coaching might focus on searching for evidence of student understanding. Focusing on the assessment of learning sometimes helps teachers understand the heart of the matter more profoundly than focusing on lesson planning does.

What specifically are you interested in working on together?
This question focuses on the specific work you will embark on and allows you to prioritize your goals. Asking what the teacher's agenda is begins the process of setting mutual goals and sets the tone for collaborative dialogue. The coach must establish the collaborative nature of the relationship and respect the teacher's goals, as well as add to those goals the things the teacher may not have identified. For example, the teacher may want to work toward improving her or his questioning techniques and the coach may suggest that the goal be broadened to the domain of classroom discourse. In this way, the focus would encompass the teacher's questions, the students' responses, and the teacher's responses to the students. It can be further broadened to include student-to-student discourse, which begins to push the envelope to developing a learning community. This in turn entails working with students to develop and self-manage their discourse skills. This broader focus is likely to affect many aspects of classroom life because its underpinnings are three principles of learning: accountable talk, socializing intelligence, and self-management of learning.

If a teacher is unclear about where to focus the work, the coach can offer a menu of suggestions and let the teacher select the starting place. The main areas correspond to the ones explained in the section on diagnosing teacher needs. For example, the coach might ask whether the teacher would like to begin with a focus on implementing the new curriculum materials, on assessing student understanding, or on a specific aspect of the content, such as computational fluency. The coach might bring the Guide to Core Issues in Mathematics Lesson Design into the picture as a means to prioritize the work.

What are your major mathematical content goals for your students this year? Which aspects of the content do you feel confident teaching? Which aspects are you less secure about? Is the teacher aware of the big ideas that are crucial for the grade level? Does he or she have some overall logical sequence for the concepts to be worked on? Can he or she identify a connected network of concepts that relate to the main mathematical topic?

It would be overwhelming to ask all of these questions in one sitting, so some of the questions listed above can be raised in subsequent meetings. The point is to gather as much information as early as possible in order to sculpt the work to match the teacher's needs.

Observing a Teacher Before the Coaching Begins

Before the actual coaching sessions begin, it is a good idea for the coach to come in and observe the teacher working with the class. This gives the coach a sense of the classroom environment and routines, the teacher's teaching style, and the students' behavior patterns and attitudes. From this observation the coach can begin to formulate the initial focus of the work. This observation is not an evaluation but a "getting to know you" visit.

It is important that the coach understand and respect the teacher's comfort level. In some schools, visitation among teachers is not a common occurrence. In some schools, working with a mentor or coach means there is something wrong with your teaching and you need help. In other schools, there is a star mentality in which competition among teachers is the norm. A competitive environment is not conducive to a learning environment. In a learning environment everyone is working to improve the collective skill level of all involved. Whether the coach is invited to observe a lesson depends not only on the teacher's comfort level, but also on the norms and culture of the school. A coach must be sensitive to these things and have a flexible repertoire of places to begin. If the coach begins by observing a lesson in the classroom, it is still advisable to have a brief talk time before the observation so that the coach can be informed about the teacher's goals and objectives. If that is not possible, questions regarding what the teacher wanted to accomplish can be asked after the observation. It is essential that the coach refrain from making assumptions about the lesson and use the post-conference dialogue to reflect on specific events or classroom discourse before offering conjectures, thereby maintaining a stance of inquiry during the debriefing conversation.

Getting Started

Scheduling and formats are logistics that need to be negotiated. How often and when will we be working together? Will we have time for both pre- and postconferences on a regular basis? If not, which conference is preferred? If we have time allotted only for a preconference, how will we give each other feedback? If we have time allotted only for a postconference, how will we share the planning?

Staff development without talk time is generally ineffective. It is important to establish that time to talk about the work is nonnegotiable. Planning time during the school day is very precious, and it is rare that you will have both a pre- and a postconference on a regular basis. In our experience, if you can have only one talk time, it is generally preferable to opt for the preconference.

The Preconference—Planning the Lesson

Often the act of lesson planning is a good place to begin the work of coaching. A preconference focused on lesson planning gives the coach an opportunity to get insight into the teacher's planning habits. The Framework for Lesson Design and Analysis (Figure 1–1) and the Guide to Core Issues in Mathematics Lesson Design (Figure 1–3) are helpful mental maps. Is the teacher clear about the mathematical focus of the lesson? Has she or he actually done the activity or the problem? Does the activity chosen align with the stated lesson goal? Is the teacher using the curriculum text as a script? Is the teacher creating her or his own lessons? If so, what is the rationale for creating the given lesson and where does it fall in a sequence of lessons? Is the teacher using a variety of resources or bound to one series? If the teacher is using a variety of resources, what is guiding the choice of activities? Do the activities revolve around important mathematical concepts? Is the teacher considering the students in the class? Does the teacher know the students well? Does the teacher underestimate or overestimate what the students are capable of? Does the teacher seem to understand how children learn mathematics and the kinds of things they might say or do to demonstrate their developing knowledge? The coach does not necessarily ask all of these questions, but rather listens to the teacher's plan to get a sense of what aspects of planning the teacher is already incorporating and what aspects may be introduced over the course of time.

Teaching the Lesson

There are three basic formats for sharing responsibility for teaching a collaboratively planned lesson: the coach teaches the lesson, the coach and teacher coteach, or the teacher teaches the lesson. A coach might initially invite the teacher to select which of these formats would be most comfortable as a starting place. Eventually all three formats can be used, depending on the focus of the given lesson. All of these formats ideally include pre- and postconferences.

The Coach Teaches the Lesson

At the school level, the coach is a potential team player with a unique challenge. She is an outsider inviting people to both "play" with her and allow her to lead. Her power to influence is "with" others, not "over" others. By rolling up her sleeves and engaging in the messy business of classroom practice, she maintains both credibility and humility. She holds her practice out for scrutiny again and again as a way to entice others to do the same. The most respected coaches "walk their talk" and as a result are instrumental in cocreating vibrant professional communities.

It is essential for coaches to be willing and able to teach children in the classrooms in which they assist teachers. It is often useful for a coach to teach a lesson or even the first few lessons in a given classroom in order to gain credibility and to set the stage for the kind of instruction she has in mind. (Other teachers can be encouraged to observe these lessons.)

We do not advocate that coaches do all the teaching; rather, it should be one of a repertoire of coaching practices. Yet we also recognize the reality that the staff developer teaching the lesson is the most popular format for a good portion of the first year that staff developers work at a school. The key to effective use of this format is that the teacher must participate in the planning and debriefing and must actively observe the lesson. For example, active observation might include noting every question the staff developer asked of students in order to examine the role of questioning in a good mathematics lesson. When a coach teaches a lesson, the coach and the teacher should have a debriefing about the lesson in the same way that they would if the classroom teacher had taught the lesson. The message is "We are here to learn from each other in the real, complex world of teaching." However, modeling lessons for the teacher should not be the only format a coach makes use of. For the coach to more fully assist teachers in practice it is necessary to move to the formats described in the next two sections.

Coteaching

The second format used in Content-Focused Coaching is one in which teacher and coach share the responsibilities for implementing a lesson. This format is rarely a starting place, though it can be. It takes trust and excellent communication skills, and it is a very effective format. For example, a teacher may feel comfortable presenting a problem to students, but less secure about facilitating whole-group conversation after the students have solved the problem. The coach might agree to facilitate the class meeting in this case. During the preconference the coach and the teacher can discuss what the teacher's focus should be during the class meeting in order for the teacher to gain confidence in facilitating student discussions of mathematics content.

Another coteaching scenario is one in which the teacher and the coach work side-by-side during small-group work time, working with individual students or small groups of students as they work through the assignment. The coach may observe the teacher's interactions and offer immediate feedback, or vice versa. Teachers often feel unclear about what constitutes appropriate interventions with students who are struggling or students who need to be challenged. By working side-by-side during this part of the class period, teacher and coach can build a set of explicit intervention strategies that the teacher can use when the coach is not present.

The Teacher Teaches the Lesson

Once coaching has been established in the school, observing the implementation of coplanned lessons is a common format for Content-Focused Coaching. Classroom observation skills are required of coaches (and teachers) if assessment of teaching and learning is to drive instruction. In this case, assessment of both teaching and learning is guiding the coaching sessions. If the Guide to Core Issues in Mathematics Lesson Design is used in planning lessons, coach and teacher will be addressing content, pedagogy, and evidence of student learning. The coach needs to document evidence of student learning or confusion while observing the lesson. Notes about what students say during classroom discourse are a source of information that allow the teacher and coach to reflect on student learning during the postconference. In addition, the coach should document the questions the teacher posed and the notations that the teacher made on the blackboard. This type of data is a source for reflecting on the effectiveness of the pedagogy. The more specific the data, the more useful.

In the following we provide some exemplary perspectives—related to the Core Issues—for observing lessons.

Is there evidence that important mathematics is at the core of the lesson and that the teacher understands the content? One thing to look for is the visuals or models the teacher has prepared or improvises to explain a concept. Another is whether the teacher has given a clear and accessible summary of concepts that students have been grappling with in the course of a lesson. A third is the teacher's ability to respond to unexpected student questions or insights. Can the teacher discern between important mathematical conjectures and superficial or tangential ones? What generalizations, if any, have the teacher or the students posited?

What is the nature of the interactions between teacher and students and among students? Are people respectful when they speak to one another? Are students confident and comfortable in raising questions, sharing ideas, and working together? Who is doing most of the talking? Is the teacher asking probing questions and giving students time to think? Are students talking to each other about their ideas, or does the dialogue always follow a teacher-student-teacher-student pattern? How do people react to mistakes or wrong answers? What, specifically, do students state or ask that shows understanding or misunderstanding of the content under discussion? These are examples of questions that can be used to analyze the degree of accountable talk in the class.

It is important to take copious and specific notes on what is actually said in a discussion in order to be able to reflect on the lesson in detail afterward. It is useful to collect student work, and especially student writing, in relation to the mathematics that may have been generated during the lesson in order to determine next steps. Many coaches do not take specific-enough notes, resulting in debriefing conferences that are too general to effect change.

To what extent does the teacher use visual aids and models to make public and facilitate student understanding? For example, the blackboard and the overhead projector are instructional tools that need to be considered carefully in lesson design because they serve different functions. Blackboards provide a lot of contiguous space, so solutions can be viewed simultaneously for comparison. The teacher can model good note-taking skills on the blackboard. It is helpful to make a sketch of what was written on the blackboard during the lesson in order to reflect on whether it helped or hindered students' understanding. An overhead projector is useful, for example, when manipulatives are going to be part of the lesson and a teacher or student needs to demonstrate with objects that are too small to be seen by everyone unless they are projected onto a large screen. These details need to become part of what a coach observes when watching a lesson in order to be cognizant of choices when planning lessons.

Are there grouping structures or modified sets of tasks to address individual student needs? Has the teacher thought about which children and how many children should work together on a specific task? Has consideration been given to the accessibility of the problem for each of the learners? Do the tasks pose an appropriate range of challenge?

What management style is being employed and is it conducive to the development of a learning community? Do children have an opportunity to reflect on their behavior and work ethic and to assess their academic achievement, or are they simply expected to follow directions and keep quiet? Do students have input into how they will monitor their behavior and improve their achievement levels? Do the teacher's decisions lead to student autonomy or dependency? It will be easier to get students to think, reason, and problem solve in math if they are thinking, reasoning, and problem solving in many areas of their lives.

Do the room arrangement and placement of supplies help or hinder the learning goals? Is the room arrangement conducive to collaborative work and does it also provide some private spaces for students who may need to work independently? Is the room neat and organized in a way that promotes autonomy? Who controls access to supplies? Are mathematician's tools—calculators, rulers, compasses, protractors, etc.— available? Are a variety of manipulative materials available?

If the necessary equipment is not available, the staff developer may have to find ways of getting them for the teacher. Removing obstacles is an important coaching move. Going to bat for the teacher with the principal or district is a way to win friends and make progress. Many a staff developer loans personal materials to colleagues in order to keep the work moving forward.

The Postconference

Ideally, the coach and teacher meet shortly after the lesson while memories are still fresh. It is helpful to take a few minutes between the lesson and the postconference to reread and make sense of notes taken. This also allows the person who taught the lesson to jot down his or her thoughts. The coach will tentatively prioritize the main issues to be addressed in the conference.

Beginning the dialogue by asking the teacher to reflect on the lesson first is generally a good move, and allows the teacher to express his or her feelings and to develop the habits of self-monitoring and self-reflection. It gives the teacher a sense of control over his or her own learning and the course of the postconference. Giving a teacher the opportunity to be the first to raise issues, concerns, or questions related to the lesson allows the coach to recognize points of agreement and to address issues that are genuinely important to the teacher. This move also prevents the coach from jumping right in with statements that may sound critical or judgmental to the teacher. Often, the teacher is a more severe critic of his or her practice than the coach is.

The main purpose of the postconference is to reflect on the lesson from a perspective of student learning. A strong focus on student learning also helps deflect the tendency to criticize teachers with respect to superficial aspects of implementing particular methods. Teaching moves are discussed as much as possible in relation to evidence of student learning. For example, if students seemed confused or reticent to answer a particular set of questions, the coach and the teacher could analyze the wording of the questions with respect to clarity and intent (assuming the coach took copious, verbatim notes). The more specific the coach's feedback in relating teaching moves and student learning, the more likely it will be useful to the teacher.

Ways to know what the teacher is learning in a postconference are to ask him or her to paraphrase suggestions offered by the coach and to invite the teacher to verbalize his or her questions and new insights. Teachers ought to feel free to question, modify, or even reject suggestions offered by a coach. What matters is the quality of reasoning manifested in such joint deliberations on the design of lessons and teaching moves that assist student learning.

Whenever possible, student work should be brought to the postconference for analysis and guidance in planning the next lesson. When studying samples of student work, the coach and the teacher focus on student understanding of the mathematics. They can ask whether the task and the assignment were clearly presented as evidenced by the quality of the work. Did the teacher clearly communicate his or her expectations? They could ask questions about student understanding of the mathematics based on the various solution strategies, types of errors, and range of responses found in the student work. All of the information gathered guides the planning of the next lesson. And as always, it is a good idea for the coach to ask the teacher how he or she can be most helpful in relation to planning the next day's lesson.

In the real world of school life, it is not always possible to have a meeting with a teacher after the lesson. When this occurs, it is good practice for the coach to give the teacher his or her notes on the lesson. If the notes had not been written with the intention to give them to the teacher after the lesson the coach should take the time to rewrite the notes and take into account that written communication is more exacting than verbal communication. It is important that the teacher receives feedback and comments that are not likely to be misconstrued as judgmental or evaluative. The notes are written in the same spirit, as the conversation would be guided by: We are colleagues doing our best to collaboratively improve the teaching and learning of mathematics in this classroom. The more specific the notes the better. It is useful to clearly indicate opinions, suggestions, or questions from the coach and to separate these from descriptions of classroom discourse. Sometimes, just providing a teacher with a clear, unedited description of what occurred in a pivotal teaching episode is most useful.

Evidence of Progress

Over the course of the year, the coach will need to document evidence of progress. It is important to think about what might constitute progress early on and to make the benchmarks of progress clear and explicit to all concerned parties. Most people tend to think about progress in terms of improved student test scores. Though this is an important piece of data, it has many limitations. First, test scores for standardized high-stakes tests only come out once a year, often at the very end of the year. We need to assess progress throughout the year. Second, test scores are just one indicator that students are progressing. Often in the first year of an initiative, test scores are not affected; they may even dip slightly as people transition from one curriculum or methodology to another. Coaches and teachers need to consider other ways of collecting data about student performance, such as student writing in the subject area or specific assignments that will double as assessments.

Change in teacher behavior and thinking is the second area to consider. Assessing teacher progress is not the same as evaluating teacher performance in the traditional meaning of the word. While formal evaluation is the job of the principal, the coach needs to look for signs that the coaching is productive. Sometimes these signs are small and can be overlooked when people are engaged in the work. All the information the coach collected when diagnosing the teacher's needs can be translated into benchmarks for progress. For example, if a teacher who once hated math is beginning to look forward to teaching it, that's progress. If a teacher only wanted the coach to model lessons and is now willing to coteach a lesson, that's progress. If a teacher once doubted that the students were capable of talking and listening to each other about important mathematics, but now believes it possible and is beginning to consider ways to increase student discourse, that's progress. If a teacher used to follow the curriculum guide as if it were gospel and is now making slight variations based on students' needs, that's progress. If the teacher is beginning to ask students what they think and to provide explanations in their own words, that's progress. If yelling and shushing were the predominant management techniques and now there are clear expectations about behavior and strategies for managing behavior that involve student self-management, that's progress. If a teacher simply did not understand that there is more to mathematics than memorizing facts, but is now willing to go a bit more deeply into the reasoning behind a procedure, that's progress. If a teacher thought the only thing that mattered was high test scores and is now beginning to realize that it is possible to maintain high test scores *and* develop deeper understanding of mathematics, that's progress.

Substantive change can also be seen in various ways that are more related to lesson design. Substantial change indicators would include a teacher internalizing the core issues of lesson design expressed in the Guide to Core Issues in Mathematics Lesson Design. For example, when a teacher begins to come to preconferences having done the mathematics activity and names more specific concepts, skills, and applications of the problem, that is significant progress. When a teacher begins to habitually ask, "What is the mathematics?" and is not satisfied with broad definitions such as "multiplication," but rather wants more specific answers, such as "the distributive property of multiplication," that's progress. When a teacher starts to independently speculate about the phrasing of questions; what visuals to use; what aspects of the lesson may be difficult for students to grasp; and how to give students entry into the mathematics—without prompting from the coach—real, enduring progress has been made.

A staff developer has to become a detective for progress. And progress should be recognized and celebrated. This is a key to improvement. This is long-term, complex work that is difficult to maintain until it becomes part of the professional culture. All steps in this direction should be noted and built on.

Change is not linear in nature. It often happens in spurts, then peters out and needs to be infused with new formats, new structures, new focuses, and the like. When energy seems to be waning, it is important to make the time to take stock and make midcourse changes that will reinspire people.

Maintaining Progress

One way to ensure that teachers will want to continue the work is to ask which things you are doing are useful and what you might need to do that you hadn't thought of. It is not only the teacher who must be accountable—accountability is reciprocal. The hardest thing for some coaches to ask is "How am I doing?" "What can I do to improve my end of the work?" It feels threatening. You are vulnerable. What if the teacher says something you don't want to hear? Ironically, it is exactly this kind of move that has the greatest impact on the relationship. If someone tells you that they need something other than what you have been offering, you have a good chance to renegotiate the work in a way that will be more productive for both of you. It feels a lot worse to find out at the end of the year that a teacher wasn't satisfied about some aspect of the work but did not feel comfortable raising the issue.

On the other hand, it is a good idea to ask the teacher, "What did you learn from this coaching session that you can generalize and use beyond this lesson?" In this way, you make what was learned explicit, and you do so on the teacher's terms. The teacher's answer may be an example of progress that you had not even imagined.

Building a Professional Community

Professional relationships are complex—and relationships are key. If colleagues enjoy each other, working together is usually easy; if disagreements arise, there is intrinsic motivation to resolve them in a win/win fashion. Respecting each other's differences and allowing those differences to become the grist for growth can be challenging. In professional relationships, the willingness to see this challenge as an opportunity can lead to innovative and profound changes in practice. For example, one teacher believes that students learn best when they sit quietly and are called on when they raise their hands. Another teacher believes that children thrive when they can converse with their classmates as they grapple with confusing and complex ideas. It would be ideal if both teachers could consider the grain of truth in each perspective: There are situations in which each belief may be true. All too often, one person tries to convince the other that they have found "the truth" and discount the possibility that what is true in one case may not be true in another. This attitude is one sure way to shut down communication and lose momentum in professional community building. If lines of communication can be kept open, there is a good chance that shared coherent views can be created over the long haul. In the short term, people can get as far as to agree to disagree; at worst each continues to try to convince the other that they are right and the other is wrong. The coach's job is to create conditions in which various views can be considered and evidence of student learning becomes the bottom line criteria for validity. Keeping conversations focused on evidence of learning makes coach and teacher less likely to get bogged down in rhetoric and more likely to make progress. The coach should view herself not as the teacher's only hope, but as more of a pragmatic architect ready to build the unique bridge that will lead to an enthusiastic and self-sustaining professional learning community at a particular school.

Teachers are going to have different reactions to coaches, and vice versa. They will bring different levels of skill to the collaboration process. Some will have difficulty working with colleagues with whom they may have a negative history. The difference between coaches and teachers is that the coach is invested in creating working relationships, while teachers appear to have the option of not getting involved. This dynamic is often difficult for new coaches. A coach who has a fear of rejection or takes things personally will have to overcome those tendencies. This is a great opportunity for personal growth if the coach shifts perspective from "it's about me" to "it's all about the work—it's not personal." Keep the big picture and the long-term goal in mind and trust that people are a lot smarter and more caring than we often give them credit for. Many issues that arise in this work are the result of miscommunication and can be avoided if we practice listening to one another and asking questions until we are sure we understand each other.

Skillful staff development engages staff members in nonthreatening ways that help them discover what they do not know, and nurtures their willingness to learn and practice more effective methods. We can develop a healthy anxiety when we become starkly aware that the status quo is insufficiently addressing the needs of students and that our practices may be part of the problem.

All change initiatives require emotional intelligence because most of us find uncertainty unsettling and admitting imperfection often triggers high anxiety and defensive patterns. People engage in reform efforts when they see a reason to. Sometimes it is painful to realize that you have not been as successful as you imagined. Containing anxiety is also necessary and is often as simple as saying to someone, "You were doing the best you knew how and now that you know better we will work together to find ways to do better. Let's start from where we are and build from here."

In Summary

Maintaining progress is often more challenging than getting started. Building self-sustaining professional communities that are focused on improvement takes patience, courage, perseverance, emotional intelligence, and skill. Staff developers should create multiple entry points for teachers and a variety of structures that provide opportunities for teachers who are at different levels and at different points in their careers to get involved. They should recognize movement in its myriad forms. Coaches should take a stance of curiosity as they look and listen to classroom discourse; study student work; talk with students about what they are learning; and watch teachers teach and make explicit to them what is working, what is changing, and what is improving. Coaches should talk with teachers and students about practices, strategies, content, assessments, and pedagogy and ask for their views about what is working, changing, and improving in order to help teachers and students begin to self-manage their own progress. In this manner, everyone is involved in cocreating learning environments in which students thrive. Through such ongoing conversations the entire learning community will gradually become smarter about teaching and learning.

Chapter Three

The Case Studies

In Chapters Five through Seven we present and discuss specific coaching sessions. Like all examples presented in this book, the case material is based on video recordings of actual in-classroom coaching led by Lucy West. Our examples are intended to provide a guided look into the practice of Content-Focused Coaching.

We provide three examples to give a flavor of the variations coaching sessions can have. The teachers range from one in her first year of teaching to one in his eighth year. The examples also illustrate different stages in the coaching relationship. The first shows a first meeting, the second is approximately the fifth meeting, and the third is a session where the teacher and coach have been working extensively together for about a year and a half. Two of the meetings are one-on-one and the third includes observing teachers and staff developers. Content-Focused Coaching can be used in a group setting and often is.

The teachers also represent a range in relation to their understanding of and comfort level teaching mathematics. One teacher openly admits discomfort and fragile understanding, another is quite comfortable with her knowledge base, and the third appears comfortable with mathematics but the extent of her knowledge base is unclear. All three teachers are willing to learn more mathematics and the pedagogical knowledge necessary to teach it well.

A thorough understanding of the mathematics content is at the very heart of what allows for productive Content-Focused Coaching. The Guide to Core Issues in Mathematics Lesson Design (Figure 1–3) contains a number of questions asking coach and teacher to develop a clear understanding of the subject-specific content to be learned.

There are two schools represented in these sessions. Though both are located in the heart of New York City, one serves a mostly middle-class population and the other serves a very eclectic population more typical of the image many of us have of inner-city schools. The schools are similar in size, and both have strong principals who are committed to improving mathematics instruction for all students.

These case studies show all three settings that are part of a complete Content-Focused Coaching session: the preconference, the lesson, and the postconference. Extensive quotes from transcripts of the actual dialogues and classroom conversations are provided. The transcripts have been slightly edited to increase the readability of these dialogues. The reader will be guided through the complex processes of coaching by the voice of the coach. Summaries and reflections are provided from the coach's perspective as a natural way to highlight and explicate core questions of lesson design and pivotal decisions underlying the coach's actions.

To draw your attention to the relationship between the general theoretical framework guiding Content-Focused Coaching and the practices that each case illustrates, we include general statements set apart from the text by boxes. These discuss core issues of instructional design that refer to the general strategies underlying Content-Focused Coaching. The Guide to Core Issues in Mathematics Lesson Design strongly influences the coach's work by providing a map of core issues that the coach can select from as she guides the conversation and responds to the teachers. The guide is used in a highly flexible manner. It does not determine the sequence in which issues are taken up in the coaching conversations.

Chapter Four

Using the CDs

The majority of coaches in District 2 have found watching others coach to be a crucial and effective means for helping them grow and develop their own coaching skills. While watching live coaching sessions is perhaps the most powerful way to learn, video clips from sessions are also a good resource, and provide possibilities that live sessions do not. For example, it is possible to view the recorded segments a number of times and from a variety of perspectives. The CDs that accompany this book are intended to give the reader a richer picture of what we mean by Content-Focused Coaching than text alone can provide. They are intended to be opportunities for the reader to become more reflective about the practice of coaching.

Each case on a CD is divided into three main sections: pre-conference, lesson, and postconference. Each main section contains a few short segments that may be viewed and discussed or analyzed one at a time. For each case there is also a transcript for the video segments that will allow you to review the dialogue and make notes in the margins.

The simplest way to use the CDs is to watch the video segments as you read the relevant chapter. This will familiarize you with the cases and give you a fuller picture of what is happening in the session as you read the transcripts and reflections in the chapter.

The self-study process described below is designed for those who want to use the CDs in more depth. The basic idea is to use the Framework for Lesson Design and Analysis (Figure 1–1), the Guide to Core Issues in Mathematics Lesson Design (Figure 1–3), and the concept of *coaching moves* to analyze and understand the cases documented on video. We encourage you to work collaboratively with a colleague as you explore the CDs. Allot a couple of hours of uninterrupted time to do this work, and keep in mind that you will probably need more than one session to work your way through a CD.

Learning Stance

When you work with the CDs, it is crucial that you take a learning stance. It is less helpful to think about all the things you would have done and more useful to look through curious eyes at what was done. This will help you stay out of the role of critic and allow you to get a feel for the kinds of conversations that lead to the development of professional communities.

Notice where in the dialogues you feel uncomfortable. The coach may be making a move that is not natural to you or is not your style. If that is the case, ask yourself what the purpose of the move might be, whether you agree with the perceived purpose, and how you might accomplish that same end using your own style. Separating style from purpose is not always easy and is one reason that we have offered the concept of coaching moves. There are different kinds of moves that work toward the same overall goal.

Getting Ready to Watch the Video Segments

Begin by solving the mathematics problem that is at the core of the lesson being coached. Read and work through the problem given in the book. If you are inclined, expand on the problem and investigate the mathematics at a level that is interesting and challenging to you. For example, in the Sillman case, the children are asked to find two-addend combinations of eleven. You might want to find all of the two-addend combinations of eleven and of ten and twelve, or all of the two-addend combinations of all of the counting numbers to eleven. Then look for patterns and see if you can predict how many two-addend combinations there would be for the number 100. You might write an equation that expresses the generalization you have discovered. In this way, you can consider the connections this problem has to the mathematics that will be taught in later units or in higher grades. This practice helps situate the lesson in the larger context of mathematics.

The next step is to look at the Guide to Core Issues in Mathematics Lesson Design (Figure 1–3) and ask yourself some of those questions. Start with the "What is the mathematics in this lesson?" questions. In considering the lesson implementation, you need to think of a particular class at the appropriate level. We strongly recommend thinking about what misconceptions students might have in relation to the mathematics under investigation and what language they might use to express partial understanding. We have found that the questions in the guide help us uncover what we do and don't know about children's learning in relation to the concepts under investigation. At this point, you might also sketch out a lesson plan.

Once you have considered the parts of the guide that are of interest to you, turn your attention to the Framework for Lesson Design and Analysis (Figure 1–1). You have already identified the *what* aspect of the lesson by doing the mathematics and reflecting on what the concepts are. If you considered the other questions included in the guide, you have also begun to think about the *how* aspect of the lesson. The *how* is related to your knowledge and belief system about teaching and learning, which, when made explicit, address the *why* aspect of the framework. At this point, you might more explicitly deliberate *why* you were considering some of the *how* choices and see if they are in line with the principles of learning espoused in this book or with some other set of principles. In other words, identify and articulate your belief system about teaching and learning.

Working with the Video Segments and Transcripts

Now it's time to work with the CDs. Before you look at the video segments, print out a copy of the transcript to keep in front of you as you watch. Before you view the preconference, review the Guide to Core Issues in Mathematics Lesson Design again and select one section that you intend to focus on when you listen to the dialogue. For example, if you choose the section "Where does this lesson fall in this unit and why?" read all of the bullets under that heading. Then watch one segment of the preconference and listen for references in the dialogue that pertain to that section.

You could also go about this in the opposite manner: You might first listen to a section of the dialogue and then go back over the transcript with the guide in hand and ask yourself what core issues were dealt with in the coaching conversation. One of the things you will notice is that the dialogue does not follow the sequence of the guide. The guide is a kind of map, not a script to be followed.

Proceed through each video segment of the preconference in the manner that feels most comfortable to you. Through this process you will begin to become familiar with the guide and begin to get a feel for the nature of a Content-Focused Coaching dialogue.

Studying the Lesson Segments

Before viewing the lesson, ask yourself what you want to pay attention to. Compile a list of possibilities. For example, are you interested in the questions the teacher asked or in the way she or he used visuals? Do you want to pay attention to children's thinking and find evidence of learning or of confusions and misconceptions? Keep in mind that your purpose in viewing the lesson is not to criticize or to focus on what the teacher should have done. It is an opportunity to analyze what actually happened. And it is an opportunity to take a stance of inquiry and consider how the preconference dialogue was related to, and had an impact on, the lesson.

Once you have decided on a focus, watch the first segment of the lesson. Then go through that portion of the lesson transcript and underline the parts that pertain to your focus. For example, if you chose to focus on teacher questioning, underline the questions the teacher posed. Ask yourself questions about what the teacher's purpose might have been and what actual response the question generated. We recommend first describing in your own words what was said, and only then drawing any inferences you might have with respect to the question. For example:

> The teacher asked student A to explain how student B got his solution. Student A seemed confused by the teacher's question, based on the evidence that student A first hesitated, had a puzzled look on his face, and then said, "What do you mean?"

In such a situation you may wonder if the child was confused by the question or by the way that student B solved the problem. Once you have reflected deeply on the situation, you might then ask yourself how else the teacher could have phrased the question.

The purpose of the process of describing and then questioning is to take us out of our habitual tendency to jump directly to global judgment and then offer advice. Our intention is to change this tendency in order to develop the habits of inquiry and the good listening and observation skills that are necessary for effective coaching. Many of us do not even realize when we are being critical or using language that could trigger a defensive reaction. It is helpful to view the tapes with an eye toward how judgmental statements can be reframed as sincere questions. This practice helps to validate whether or not the inferences were accurate. In coaching, such a practice is a prerequisite to engaging in genuine dialogue and avoiding defensive reactions.

Studying the Postconference

After you have worked with all of the segments of the lesson in the manner described above, you are ready to consider the postconference. Ask yourself, "What issues might I raise with this teacher if given the opportunity?"

When preparing to view the postconference, refer once again to the Guide to Core Issues in Mathematics Lesson Design. Mark the questions that pertain to the issues you feel are relevant for discussion. Turn to the video segments and begin the same process that was described for viewing the preconference: Watch the dialogue and listen for which core issues were discussed. The difference here is that you have some ideas of your own that you can include as you consider what was and was not addressed in the postconference. Finally, spend a few minutes speculating on what the teacher may have learned that is specific to the lesson under discussion, and to the practice of teaching and learning in general, as a result of these coaching episodes.

Studying Coaching Moves

If you go through the video segments of a coaching case a second time, you might more specifically focus on the interactive role of the coach, paying attention to the moves the coach is making. How does the coach help the teacher foster student learning in the lesson coached? How does the coach help the teacher develop teaching expertise in general? In what ways does the coach address core questions and issues of lesson design and analysis?

In order to reflect on the dialogical and coconstructive nature of the coaching dialogue, we differentiate two basic kinds of discursive coaching moves: moves that invite the teacher to verbalize his or her perceptions, thoughts, plans, deliberations, and arguments and moves through which the coach provides direct assistance relevant to the planning and implementation of the lesson design. Ask yourself: When is the coach offering suggestions, and when is she or he soliciting ideas from the teacher? Who seems to be guiding this session? Who is making the final choices about what will and will not be included in the lesson? Where does the interaction between these two kinds of moves lead to instances in which teacher and coach constructively contribute toward designing and implementing lessons that are conducive to student learning? In other words, you can go through a process similar to the one described in relation to the Framework for Lesson Design and Analysis and the Guide to Core Issues in Mathematics Lesson

Design, but now focused specifically on the kind of coaching moves used to get at these issues.

There are many more perspectives from which to view the CDs. You can view them from the perspective of the principles of learning, for example. The principle of *accountable talk* is one of the easiest to start with. You might listen to the coaching dialogue for evidence that the talk is accountable to mathematics, to pedagogy, and to the relationship. You could view the lesson for evidence of students' accountable talk as well. Reread the sections in the book that pertain to the principle you wish to explore, then watch the tapes or read the transcripts with that principle in mind. This process will help you become familiar with the principles of learning and what you are looking for in practice.

It is our sincere intention that you find a multitude of ways to interact with the CDs that will assist you on your journey in the exciting and complex world of teaching and learning and the Content-Focused Coaching of teachers.

Chapter Five

Coaching a New Teacher:
The Case of Kathy Sillman

The School

Public School 234 is an elementary school in south Manhattan in New York City. The school serves a neighborhood population that is largely upwardly mobile; the parents tend to be highly educated and involved. It serves students in prekindergarten through grade five. The school is rooted in a progressive philosophy of education. From its inception more than twenty years ago, teachers employed instructional practices such as cooperative learning in heterogeneous classes; integrated curriculum focusing on theme-based units of study; and learning through primary source materials, projects, field trips, and hands-on experiences. Most of the staff at PS 234 has participated in content-focused in-classroom staff development.

The Teacher

Though this was Kathy Sillman's first year as a head classroom teacher in a public school, Kathy had worked for a year in a private school where she cotaught a third-grade class. Kathy had extensive student teaching experience in graduate school. During the summer prior to beginning her teaching assignment at PS 234, Kathy attended a one-week institute focused on math teaching and learning and on the new curriculum materials the school was using.

It is unclear how strong Kathy's mathematics content knowledge is, yet she is quite open to learning mathematics. She loves children and is naturally inquisitive about how they think and work. She observes her students closely and carefully and uses these observations to guide her instructional choices. Her management style is respectful of students and gives them the opportunity to make choices for themselves. Kathy thinks through her lessons and is willing to put in the necessary time to plan and prepare. She is still relatively new to teaching and has not yet developed a large repertoire of teaching and assessment strategies. She is engaged in figuring out how to use the written curriculum materials in the *Investigations in Numbers, Data, and Space* program. Kathy understands that the curriculum materials are there to guide her instruction and ensure that she focuses on the important concepts for the grade level. She is working on her capacity to make appropriate decisions for her class in relation to the activities described in the text.

The Class

Kathy is teaching a kindergarten/first-grade "bridge" class. The class consists of twenty-six students, half kindergarteners and half first graders. Kathy will have her kindergarten students for two years. They will become her first graders next year when a new group of kindergarten students enters the school. This arrangement is designed to build community and to allow teachers to get to know their students very well. This is her class's first year with Kathy as their teacher.

The students have a range of understanding that is typical of any group of twenty-six five- and six-year-old people. Many are articulate and openly inquisitive about mathematics, while others are shy and in need of support and direction when they engage in mathematics activities. A few students seem to be advanced in their knowledge of numbers and have a natural tendency to look for patterns and make connections and generalizations. Others do not yet have one-to-one correspondence and are still learning to conserve number. It is early December, and Kathy and her class have settled into routines that are designed to give children both structure and freedom.

The Lesson

This lesson is "Eleven Fruits." The teachers' curriculum material state the heart of the task:

> You have eleven fruits in your basket, some are one kind of fruit, and the rest are another kind. How many of each could you have?

(Mathematical Thinking at Grade 1. *Investigations in Number, Data, and Space*. Kilman, Russell, Wright, Mokros 1998, 93)

What Is the Mathematics in the Lesson?

This problem is classified in the curriculum materials as a "How many of each?" problem. This type of problem gives students a target number and asks them to find combinations of addends that sum to the target number, in this case eleven. These problems have several answers and also present the opportunity to explore and become familiar with several mathematical concepts and ways of reasoning. There are many concepts and skills related to this task, including counting and keeping track of a set of objects; combining two quantities (addition); part/part/whole relationships; decomposing quantities; finding combinations of eleven; and representing solutions to problems using numbers, pictures, or words.

The problem is set in a real-world context that can be modeled and discussed. For example, some given strawberries and some given bananas can be referred to as a particular set of fruits; hence combining the set of strawberries and the set of bananas results in the more abstract and larger set of fruits. In numeric reasoning, a basic mathematical concept is that all counting numbers except number one, are additive compositions of other numbers. A given number can thus be decomposed into smaller numbers that when joined together add up to the original number. These types of problems thus invite an exploration of the part/part/whole relationships of a given number.

In addition, depending on the constraints given, the problem presents an opportunity to become familiar with the commutative property of addition. If the problem is presented with the constraint that students can use only two addends of eleven, the commutative property can be brought to the fore. The commutative property demonstrated in $5 + 6 = 6 + 5 = 11$ is important to understand and apply in addition. The order in which we add two numbers does not affect the result of the operation. Noticing what is the same and what is different about these number sentences allows children to articulate the idea that the total is the same in both cases, but the addends are reversed. In the same way, the sequence in which different kinds of fruit are added to a bowl does not affect the quantitative result. In the context of this problem, there are two kinds of fruits being combined, for example, strawberries and bananas, highlighting the idea that five strawberries and six bananas is a different combination than six strawberries and five bananas. When the quantity of each type of fruit is reversed, the total sum of the fruits remains the same.

Consideration of the question "What are all the possible ways of combining two fruits to get a total of eleven fruits?" is useful in thinking about the strategies that students might use to find multiple solutions to the problem. For example, compensation is a mental arithmetic strategy that many students construct naturally as they encounter various arithmetic problems. Children notice that "if you take one off of one addend and give it to the other," the sum remains the same (Fosnot and Dolk 2001a, 98). This strategy becomes especially powerful when adding large numbers, such as $358 + 499$. Applying the strategy of compensation, the problem becomes $357 + 500$, which is easy to add mentally. Moreover, the problem can be used to introduce students to the importance of systematic organization and to a search for pattern. "How do we know we have them all?" is an important mathematical question that can be applied to these problems.

Considering the mathematical ideas related to a problem prepares teachers to understand students' related ideas and puts them in a better position to address their students' varying needs. In addition, by thinking about the network of concepts that are related to any given problem, the teacher can become more cognizant of how the activities at earlier grade levels lay the foundation for the mathematics taught in subsequent years. Even a problem like this contributes to building the foundation for algebra, in this case by allowing students to become familiar with commutativity.

Where Does This Lesson Fall in This Unit and Why?

The "Eleven Fruits" investigation is the third "how many of each" task presented in the unit Mathematical Thinking at Grade 1 *(Investigations, in Number, Data, and Space)*. The activity is recommended as an "assessment" to give the teacher an opportunity to observe how students find at least one combination of eleven. The teacher is told to decide what problem students will solve. Recommendations include choosing one number that the entire class will explore, and giving specific numbers to individual students to increase or decrease the challenge level of the problem. The suggestions for determining what problem students will solve give the teacher a large terrain of concepts to choose from. There is no discussion of the repercussions of the choices in terms of what mathematics will become more or less visible with each choice. The teacher can decide that all students will work with the same two objects (such as peas and carrots), with any two objects that fall within a given category (fruit), or with any two objects at all (marbles and buttons). It is recommended that children first work on finding two-addend combinations of the target number, but some students might be allowed to include solutions using three addends.

The curriculum text attempts to engage the teacher in a kind of dialogical process that requires the teacher to interact with the curriculum in a manner that is neither completely open-ended nor strictly scripted. The text nudges the teacher into deciding what mathematics will be focused on based on students' prior knowledge. In this regard, the text is in line with the kind of professional thinking that Content-Focused Coaching aims to initiate, assist, and develop.

History of the Coaching Relationship

This coaching session is the very first between Lucy West and Kathy Sillman. It took place in December. The preconference lasted about twenty-five minutes, the lesson forty-five minutes, and the postconference about twenty minutes. The preconference took place about an hour before the lesson would be taught.

The Preconference

Walking into the session, I do not know what lesson we will be teaching, as we had not had an opportunity to speak before the session. In the reality of school life, this is often the case. This is not ideal, as the coach can be more helpful if he or she has prior information about and has given thought to the lesson and the unit.

> To collaboratively assist a teacher's lesson at hand, and to foster in the long run the teacher's professional growth, it is pivotal for the coach to respectfully get to know the teacher's thinking, knowledge, and beliefs.

In this case, I enter the coaching session with no prior thoughts about a specific lesson design. I am relying on Kathy to describe her lesson goal and plan, and I will use my experience and knowledge about teaching and the development of mathematical thinking to address core issues of lesson design. This provides for a kind of natural window into the teacher's thinking and knowledge base. It also helps to establish the collaborative nature of the work. My role here is to assist the teacher, who maintains her "ownership" of the lesson. Based on what I learn from her, I will make suggestions and point out possible pitfalls, but the final choices will be Kathy's. Especially in a first coaching session, it is important that the working relationship be established from a place of mutual respect and trust. Teachers may have weak mathematical content knowledge, but they have knowledge about their students, their prior mathematical experiences, and their class routines.

The first few minutes of the session are spent in gathering information from Kathy that will give me a sense of her situation and experience. I first invite Kathy to tell me about herself and her experience as a teacher. This helps put her at ease and also gives me useful information. With respect to her work at PS 234, Kathy explains that she has been collaborating with the teachers on her grade level to make the best use of the curriculum units with "bridge" classes. Kathy tells me that she sometimes has children work in small groups that contain both first-grade and kindergarten students and that she sometimes has them work in small groups where all students are in the same grade. At times the class works as a whole group. When I press Kathy about how she makes these grouping decisions, she tells me that she bases her decisions on assessment.

Lucy: So when you're thinking about mathematics, you're actually thinking about two separate curriculums?

Kathy: At times. I mean, that's the tricky part—you know—how are we going to do that? And sometimes there are two lessons going on at once, and sometimes the two lessons have some of the first graders in one of the lessons and some of the kindergarteners in one of the lessons, depending on where they're at, and sometimes everyone's doing the same thing.

Lucy: When you say "depending on where they're at," are you thinking about where the students are at mathematically? Because you said sometimes you're mixing K and 1.

Kathy: Right. As far as I've been able to assess.

Lucy: Okay. And what kinds of assessments are you using or doing to determine that?

Kathy: Observations of how they're doing different activities. Looking at the way that they're recording their ideas. Looking at how they're thinking about problems and approaching problems. How many different solutions they can find to one problem. How they can explain what they're doing.

Lucy: That sounds great.

I am impressed by Kathy's description of her observation assessments and curious about the extent of her knowledge. I make a note to explore assessment with Kathy in a future coaching session. I turn the conversation to the day's lesson by asking Kathy to tell me about the lesson she is planning. She explains that the "Eleven Fruits" problem, which will be today's assignment, reminds her of the peas-and-carrots problem that the children worked on some weeks ago. She explains that she had changed the context of the peas-and-carrots problem to red apples and green apples because the children had been studying apples. We discuss her lesson plan for the "Eleven Fruits" problem.

Lucy: So tell me about this one.

Kathy: It's a project where they're working on finding combinations of the number eleven, but it's open ended in terms of . . . the context is a fruit salad. And they can choose the types of fruit that they're using. They can only choose two to begin with. . . . The tricky part is how to word it. It's eleven fruit total. How many of each of two different kinds of fruit? And hopefully, I'll be able to model that a little bit with them before sending them off, so I hope they can get the idea that it's eleven total, but then they need to look for some of one and some of the other. For example, some strawberries and some bananas, but it has to equal eleven altogether.

Lucy: Which is identical to the red apples and green apples problem, except the number is changed.

Kathy: Yeah. It was a little more concrete when we did the apples because they actually had apples in front of them. They were covered with silver foil, so they couldn't see which ones were red and which ones were green. And this is a little bit—I don't have eleven things in front of me, so . . . that will be another thing, to see if they can get the same concept.

Lucy: So you're thinking about modeling it somehow, but you're not sure what you're going to use to model it with? Is that what I'm hearing? Or do you have a plan about how you would model this?

Kathy: I want to introduce it by reading this book to set the context. . . . But it's more of a counting book; it sort of builds up [Kathy reads]: "Take one yellow pineapple, two yellow bananas"—and it goes all the way through eight. And where I need to get to after this is to say, "Okay, now you all are going to be drawing or figuring out what kind of fruit salad you want to make, but you can have only eleven things."

We have reached a delicate moment in our conversation. In my view, the mathematics in the book that Kathy has so lovingly chosen does not match the mathematical inquiry she is asking her students to pursue. Especially because this is our first meeting, I want Kathy to know that I respect her ideas and am there to support her. I also want to encourage the integration of literature and mathematics. At the same time, I believe that her choice of this book might create unnecessary confusion for some of her students. My goal is for Kathy to think through the lesson from the students' perspective, which I hope will lead her to a reconsideration of this choice.

Thinking about the specifics of the intended learning in a lesson from the students' perspective is a crucial part of what Content-Focused Coaching asks for. In this preconference I do not follow the Guide to Core Issues in Mathematics Lesson Design line-by-line. Rather, I follow the natural flow of the conversation and rely on the core issues in lesson planning to guide me in focusing our conversation on important ideas in lesson design.

Lucy: Do you anticipate any confusion between this story and what you're trying to get them to do?

Kathy: I hope it will be clear. . . . We've been talking a lot about counting books and this is more of a counting book. However, when we did counting books before, they had lots of different pieces of paper and they knew they were drawing one and then two and then three . . .

Lucy: Right. But what you want them to do when you're done with this book is not a counting activity; you want them to do a combinations activity. So I'm wondering how we can make a transition that makes what you want them to do the connection. So it's kind of cool that this is a book about fruit salad and that it's got numbers in it, but the activity that's going on here is different from what you're going to ask them to do.

Kathy: Right.

Lucy: And that could be problematic, especially for kindergarten children. So we need to think a little bit about how to use this book and then what the transition needs to be to make that work. Does that make sense?

Kathy: Yeah.

Lucy: See, here, the difference between the counting and the combinations? You're working on a problem that has two constraints. The constraint is number eleven, and that there are two addends . . . so it's going to be strawberries and bananas, or whatever. So let's think about how to make the transition. Let's hold this [the book] for a minute and keep going about what happens next.

I tread as lightly as I know how in attempting to balance the tension between wanting the lesson to be successful and wanting Kathy to feel competent. I keep my tone friendly and light. I focus a bit on the mathematics because I'm not sure whether Kathy really sees the difference between counting and adding. As it turns out, putting the book aside while we ponder the rest of the lesson gives us both a chance to more deeply understand the intended learning and to reconsider Kathy's initial choice of a motivating context for the lesson problem.

> The coach remains alert to the tensions between his or her accountability for student learning and the need to have a trusting relationship with the teacher. To dogmatically instruct "good" or "successful" teaching would only increase such tensions. The skillful coach engages the teacher in a dialogue to think through critical aspects of a lesson.

Kathy goes on to explain the orchestration of the lesson. She plans to state the problem in a whole-group meeting. The students will decide on the two fruits for their salads; get paper as they leave the meeting area; and have the choice of using manipulatives such as Unifix cubes or color tiles and crayons, markers, and color pencils. She expects her students to make choices and will not require the use of particular material or approach.

I have no objections to Kathy's general scripting of the lesson. Her overall plan gives me a sense that one of her overarching goals is for her students to do their own task-related thinking and problem solving. The plan gives them a well-designed opportunity to take a few steps toward becoming autonomous learners. Our long-term educational goals seem to be similar and classroom management does not appear to be an issue. I return the conversation from questions of general pedagogy to the content-specific pedagogy of this lesson. I dance back and forth between the mathematics and the general pedagogy of the lesson because I am clear that the general script of the lesson will not present a problem and I am hoping that we can get at the mathematics by thinking about the content-specific pedagogical choices.

Lucy: The question is, do you want to model with them at all? Because one way to model would be to take the tiles or take the cubes or whatever and say, "These are strawberries and these are bananas, and we're going to make a salad." And have a bowl and throw them in the bowl, or whatever it is you want to do. So that might be one way to model, knowing that once you model it that way, a lot of kids are going to do it that way.

Kathy: Right.

Lucy: So however you model it is going to influence how they do it. So you might think about—should I model it one way? Or two ways? Because you could model it as a drawing as well. You could just model it with numbers. You can model in a variety of ways. . . . The more ways you model it, the more likely they're going to make choices that suit them, rather than imitate what you did. Does that make sense?

Kathy: It does. I guess I'm hesitant to model it at all. Just to see how they would come up with it on their own. But maybe there's nothing wrong with modeling it, if it helps them . . .

Lucy: I think there's a misconception sometimes that when you're teaching in a constructivist way, that you don't do anything, that you kind of put out the problem and that's it. But sometimes that is a misconception. The balance between what you ask kids to do and how much information you give is always a tricky balance, and it's part of the art of figuring all this stuff out.

Views on what is considered "good" practices of teaching are deeply shaped by beliefs on learning. In Content-Focused Coaching the coach addresses such underlying beliefs in relation to the learning and teaching of specific content in a lesson.

Decisions on issues such as how to begin a lesson or to what extent it is necessary to present a task are highly influenced by beliefs about teaching and learning. In my view, the teacher is guiding the trajectory of mathematical concepts students will explore. Though exploration is important, time constraints necessitate that it be fruitful and structured around important mathematical ideas. The goal is to strike a balance between providing enough information to give students access to the problem without inhibiting the way they would approach the problem without assistance. Time will be allotted for sharing strategies, and ultimately the class with the teacher's assistance may collectively determine that one strategy is more efficient than another. Students will, however, more readily engage in fruitful sharing and discussion after they have had time to explore a bit as they attempt to solve problems themselves.

At this point in our dialogue, I return the focus to the students in the class. Though Kathy's general philosophy of teaching seems to be similar to mine, the way we interpret the implications of "constructivism" is different. I am interested in getting a sense of the range of understandings that Kathy's students have demonstrated in order to help her consider ways of presenting the lesson problem.

Lucy: Let's go back to the problem with seven. When you worked on seven, was it hard for any of your students? Were any of them able to come up with only one solution to the problem?

Kathy: There's a big range, especially with the K–1. Some of them could come up with the solution, but then just recording it on paper was the challenge. Some of them could quickly find multiple solutions.

Lucy: And how did they record it? Did they just use numbers?

Kathy: Some of them used number sentences, $3 + 4 = 7$, and they could automatically see that that meant $4 + 3 = 7$.

Lucy: And did they label them, like "peas and carrots" or "red apples/green apples," or did they draw pictures, or just numbers?

Kathy: Some of them drew pictures; some of them drew numbers and then next to one number they would have a green circle; next to another number they would have a red circle.

Lucy: They were color coding.

Kathy: Right. Some of them wrote the numbers in red and green.

Kathy and I discuss her implementation of the problem. I discover that though Kathy used foil-covered red and green apples to model the "seven-ness" of the problem, she did not have students share possible solutions. I turn the conversation back to thinking about the range of students in the class.

Lucy: Are there any kids in your class who don't have one-to-one correspondence?

Kathy: I think there are a few.

Lucy: Would they have a problem with the number eleven?

Kathy: But they could go back and check to make sure.

Lucy: So, in other words, if they count a second or third time, they would get eleven?

Kathy: They could do it with seven.

Lucy: They could do it with seven. What do you think about eleven?

Kathy: I think it'll be interesting to see. I mean, I can't say for certain it's too much for them. But I think it'll definitely be interesting to see.

We are back at the question of how to begin the lesson. We agree that it should be presented to the whole group in a meeting area, but there are many other details to consider.

Lucy: So let's go by your instincts, because you've been working with the kids. What's your instinct about modeling or not? How much would you want to model?

Kathy: I think it could be helpful, maybe modeling with either the Unifix cubes or tiles, but then leaving it to them how they record the information on paper.

Lucy: Okay, and what would you do with the Unifix cubes or tiles?

Kathy: For example, maybe I would ask a child, "What two fruits could we use?" Maybe they would say, "Strawberries and bananas." And then I'd take red—"How many strawberries?"—and yellow—"How many bananas?" And check to see, do we really have eleven. How many of each?

Lucy: And then you could write on the blackboard a number sentence . . .

Kathy: Yeah, that's also the question, because I was looking in here [the teacher's guide] at the different ways they record information. And they were saying the difference between recording it just one way versus recording it in several ways.

Lucy: And were they suggesting that you model the different recordings, or that you . . . ?

Kathy: In this book, it seemed like all of that would come after the lesson, when you're collecting the data from the children.

Lucy: So what I'm hearing you say is, you don't want to record the number part of it. You just sort of want to model the activity part of it. In other words, making clear that eleven is one of the constraints and that two fruits is one of the constraints.

Kathy: Mm-hmm.

In this coaching session I do not know the curriculum unit well and am not clear why the authors of the teacher manual recommended holding off on demonstrating ways to record the number sentences that students come up with. Kathy is new to the curriculum and is following the suggestions in the text, for the most part. My inclination is to record what is being said in class by using either pictures or words, or pictures and numbers. I might even record the children's ideas in a number sentence to give them symbolic models so they can naturally start using mathematical symbols in context where appropriate. However, I decide to leave this decision to Kathy. I have not taught kindergarten or first grade and am not confident that my inclination is a good one.

I am cognizant of Kathy's concern about the range of student knowledge and want to use this session as an opportunity to help her see that there are ways of addressing the range of student needs without having to create two different activities. I return the conversation to the students' prior knowledge. Kathy and I discuss which specific children will have difficulty gaining access to the problem and which could be challenged to find all of the two-addend solutions to the problem. Becoming cognizant of the range of student understandings and the possible difficulties students may exhibit allows us to think ahead about how to create a lesson that is flexible and can be differentiated to meet the various needs of those who may struggle and those who could benefit from additional challenge. This also reminds us that each student is unique and will bring different levels of understanding and experience to the activity. Through considering each student, teachers and coaches are more likely to create lessons that encourage students to construct meaning in ways that honor their specific starting points and styles. If learning is understood to take place at the intersection of prior knowledge, experiences provided by the assigned activities, and dialogue about the content, it is reasonable to assume that each student's learning will be unique. Our job as teachers is to provide structures and ask questions that allow all students to build knowledge from where they begin. This view is different from the notion that all first graders must know the same thing at the same time. Negotiating the tension between helping students meet "standards" with the reality of individual differences is an interesting challenge. What does it mean to have standards and guidelines for all first graders when in reality little Johnny is learning to count and Suzie is already adding two-digit numbers?

Kathy and I discuss ways to support all of the students in her class. We agree that all students will be asked to find at least one way to solve the problem and that those who can do that will be encouraged to find more ways. We both think that students should work independently, because we want to use the problem as an assessment. However, we agree that it is okay if students talk with each other if they choose to as long as each child makes a record of the solutions he or she comes up with. We then discuss the four students who Kathy suspects may have trouble coming up with a solution.

Lucy: These folks you know are going to have a problem, or you think may have a problem. So I'm wondering, is there any more scaffolding or support you want to do—let's say you send everybody else off to get started, but you're worried about these four kids. Would you keep them in the meeting area for a minute or two longer, and perhaps ask them how they might record the one you just modeled?

Kathy: That's a good idea. I haven't done that, but it sounds like it might work.

Lucy: You want to give that a shot and see if it helps? So you'd have some paper in the meeting area, and you could say, "Let's do one together." So you do one together with these four kids and see if they can record the one you just modeled. And then say to them, "Can you think of another one?" And if they can think of another one, then you send them off on their own: "Okay, go off now and write the one you just thought of down." And if they can't think of another one, think about the concept of exchange: "What if I took out one strawberry and I put in another banana? Then what would I have?" You know, or something like that.

Kathy: Mm-hmm.

Lucy: So that you can push these guys who are young and not quite thinking numerically yet—maybe don't have a concept of magnitude yet—in the direction. You're giving them a little bit more scaffolding than the rest of the class needs. Does that make sense?

Kathy: Yeah.

Kathy decides to try staying behind with the four students while the rest of the class goes to work. The three students who Kathy thinks can find all twelve solutions will be challenged to do so as a group. These management structures are new for Kathy and she is a bit worried that she will lose sight of the whole if she focuses on the few.

My main concern continues to be the mismatch between the counting book that Kathy is planning to read and the problem of decomposing the number eleven into two kinds of fruits. After Kathy and I have collaboratively thought quite a bit about the intended learning and students' prior knowledge, I feel it is time to address this issue directly.

Lucy: Now I'm going to jump back here [pointing to the book]. I'm worried about this book with these kids [the children who may have difficulty understanding the problem].

Kathy: Yeah.

Lucy: So, if you are going to read this book, I think it's going to take you off your task. Even though it has the same title, the mathematics is different. Unless you wanted to make up a story about fruit salad that's more like this problem.

Kathy: Yeah, I think that would be better. Maybe I could say, "We've just had Thanksgiving, and there was a nice fruit salad for dessert, and there were only two kinds of fruit." I mean, something along those lines.

Lucy: Exactly. "It was the most amazing fruit salad. It only had two kinds of fruits, but it was so delicious. What kinds of fruits do you think it had? Name two fruits." "Yeah, those were it . . ."

Kathy: I think that would be better.

Lucy: "And the other amazing thing was that in every bowl, there was exactly eleven fruits. Is that amazing? There were two kinds and there was exactly eleven. So, do you have any idea how many strawberries and how many . . . could have been in my bowl?" So you make it very personal, put the context right into Thanksgiving, which just passed, and put it directly into the mathematics that you're heading for. Does that make sense?

Kathy: Yeah.

Kathy and I both feel good about this new idea. I end the conversation by asking Kathy how I can be of help to her. Kathy informs me that she would like assistance in conducting the whole-class discussion after the students have worked on the problem. She also indicates that it is time for her to go back to class. Time pressures are a reality. I quickly reassure Kathy that we can discuss this issue in our postconference and that it is unlikely that there will be time for a class meeting at the end of the lesson today. During our postconference, Kathy and I will have an opportunity to look at her students' work, reflect on what happened during the lesson, and consider what her next steps will be. At that time we can discuss ways to focus the follow-up meeting with students.

The Lesson

Kathy keeps to our plan. She begins the lesson in the meeting area with the children sitting in a large circle on the rug. Kathy sits cross-legged on the floor among her students and begins the lesson by telling the students a story about her family's Thanksgiving tradition.

Kathy: To get things started I wanted to tell you a little story about something that we do at my house for Thanksgiving. Because yesterday many people told me about what they do at their house for Thanksgiving, and things that they eat, and things that they do. So every day for dessert, my grandmother—it was at my grandmother's house—you know what she gives us? She gives us each our very own bowl of fruit. And it's a very special bowl, you know why? Because everybody's bowl has eleven pieces of fruit in it. But you know what else? We all have two different kinds of fruit in our bowl. So she said, "Kathy, what's your favorite kind of fruit? What kind of fruit do you want this year?" And I said, "Well, I love blueberries and I love strawberries." So guess what? I had a bowl, and I'm going to draw a circle, just so you can kind of think of my bowl. And I'm going to show you how many strawberries there were in my bowl. Can you help me count? [Kathy takes four red Unifix cubes and places them in the circle she has drawn on the paper on the rug. The students count in chorus: "One, two, three, four."] There were four strawberries in my bowl. How many blueberries could there have been? Remember, there are eleven altogether. What do you think, Miranda?

Miranda: Um . . . four more.

Kathy: Four more? Can you help me count? Sh, shh, let's count. [Counting with students]. One, two, three, four. Who can raise their hand? How can we check if this is eleven altogether? Michael?

Michael: Count.

Kathy: Will you help me? Okay, shh, let's have Michael count.

Michael: One, two, three, four, five, six, seven, eight.

As I observe the lesson I realize that Kathy and I did not discuss the example she will use. It seems to me that four may not have been the best number to begin with, because four plus seven is a more difficult combination of eleven than ten plus one or nine plus two or five plus six. I make a note that in the future I want to remember to consider the opening numbers as well as the opening question.

The second thing I realize is that Kathy is asking students again and again to "count" the number of Unifix cubes. Asking students only to count keeps them from thinking in more sophisticated ways. And from the speed with which some students called out the answer to the problem, I know that they either knew the fact that four plus four is eight or that they have other efficient ways of thinking about the problem.

> Based on what is agreed in the preconference, the coach can participate in various ways during the lesson to assist the intended student learning. A natural strategy is for the coach to take up student contributions in the classroom conversation and to help steer it on a productive course.

I know that counting through a set of objects is the most basic means of determining a sum, and I decide to quickly model other questions Kathy might ask to get her students to combine quantities more efficiently. During the preconference Kathy discussed the possibility of my intervening during the lesson and she said she would welcome the help. I use intervention as sparingly as possible and always discuss it with the teacher beforehand.

Lucy: Can I just ask a question?

Kathy: Oh. Yeah.

Lucy: Somebody said that's eight. How did you know that was eight so fast?

Student 1: 'Cause I always counted with my own fingers, 'cause I counted one, two, three, four, five, six, seven, eight.

Lucy: Uh-huh. [Gesturing to another student] And you knew it was eight very fast?

Student 2: Me?

Lucy: Yeah.

Student 2: That's because I only knew that four plus four is eight.

Lucy: Four plus four is eight. So there was lots of different ways to know that that was eight right away.

Student 3: I know it was eight because I have a book about a calculator.

Lucy: Okay . . . but we now need to get to eleven.

I hope that this intervention will demonstrate for Kathy the idea that it is better to ask students how they are calculating than to tell them only to count. Though Kathy continues asking her students to count during this meeting, I will be able to discuss this during the postconference and my intervention has "marked" the conversation during the lesson in a way that will help Kathy recall the conversation.

Though I am concerned about seeing counting as the sole addition strategy being encouraged, I was also impressed by the fact that when Miranda said to add four to four to get eleven, Kathy did not say, "no, that's wrong." She instead took the child's suggestion and then helped her to see that the sum was eight, not eleven. This led to a new problem: How many more do I need to get to eleven now that I have eight? This brought the class's attention to the problem at hand:

Kathy: We need to get to eleven . . . so what if we start at eight . . . Kika?

Kika: Um, we need three more strawberries and just one more blueberry.

Kathy: Three more strawberries . . .

Kika: I mean, two more strawberries and one more blueberry.

Kathy: Two more strawberries and one more blueberry? Let's try. Let's put in two more strawberries and one more blueberry, and then . . . will you help me count to see how many there are?

Kika: Okay.

Kathy: Go ahead.

Kika: One, two, three, four, five, six, seven, eight, nine, ten, eleven.

Kathy: There are eleven there! So if this was my bowl of fruit, how many blueberries are there? Just blueberries.

Kika: Five.

Kathy: There are five blueberries. And how many strawberries, Carson?

Carson: There's six.

Kika uses mental calculations to figure out that she needs three more pieces of fruit to get to eleven, then splits the three into a two and a one. She self-corrects when she says, "I mean, two more straw-berries and one more blueberry." This might indicate mathematical reasoning that involves more than counting objects. Kathy, however, asks Kika, "Will you help me count to see how many there are?" A better intervention would have been, "How did you know that we need two more strawberries and one more blueberry?" Or, "Can you convince us that two more strawberries and one more blueberry will give us eleven pieces of fruit?" I note this interaction in great detail because it is a concrete, specific example that I can discuss with Kathy during the postconference. This example has the potential of opening a dialogue about probing questions versus leading questions and listening to student thinking with a curious ear. Curiosity plus an understanding of the mathematics and how people develop an under-standing of mathematics provides inspiration for how to facilitate each student's learning.

Kathy's next move is to invite other solutions to the problem.

Kathy: Let's hear one more way. Andrew?

Andrew: You could take a strawberry away and put in another blueberry because it's just the opposite of the color.

Kathy: Wow! Let's try that. . . . I'm gonna take away a strawberry, I'm gonna put in a blueberry. Do you think there's still eleven?

Some Students: Yeah.

Kathy: You think so? Can you help me count? One, two, three, four, five, six, seven, eight, nine, ten, eleven. Oh, you're right, that's amazing!

Andrew uses the strategy of compensation that was mentioned briefly in the preconference and discussed in the mathematics section of this chapter. This is a natural approach to thinking about combinations and one that many students discover independently. Kathy again inter-venes by asking for a count instead of asking Andrew to convince the class that there will still be eleven.

Nathaniel is invited to share his idea:

Kathy: Ok, Nathaniel, what?

Nathaniel: You can know, like, six and six is twelve, so just take away one blueberry or strawberry and then that'll make, like, twelve.

Kathy: That's another way to do it. Absolutely.

Nathaniel: Make eleven.

Here Nathaniel is making the connection to a "doubles minus one" strategy ($6 + 6 = 12$; therefore, $6 + 6 - 1 = 11$) for finding the combi-nation five plus six equals eleven. It appears to me that Kathy under-stands the child's thinking but misses an opportunity to clarify that thinking for the class. Doubles plus or minus one or two is another important and natural strategy that children develop for finding combinations of numbers and learning basic facts. Remembering that Kathy is interested in assessing her students and using the information gleaned to guide her instruction, I make note of these interactions so I can think about ways of helping Kathy meet her goal.

Carson brings forth a third strategy for finding combinations of numbers.

Kathy: Carson?

Carson: It's just the opposite.

Kathy: Tell me what you mean.

Carson: I mean if there were six strawberries and 5 blueberries, you just take away one strawberry and put another blueberry—it would be the opposite.

Kathy: So are you saying that six strawberries and five blueberries is the same thing as five strawberries and six blueberries?

Carson: Yeah.

It would have been better to ask, "So are you saying that six strawberries and five blueberries gives you the same total of fruits as five strawberries and six blueberries?" That would lead to thinking about how the total remains eleven when the addends are reversed.

Kathy is already open to hearing many ideas and strategies and validating student thinking. She is curious about how students reason. It is only a matter of time and focus before Kathy's questions will invoke rigorous, exciting discussions about important mathematics. I am really excited at having the opportunity to work with her.

A couple of students express some confusion during the meeting. One is Nadia, a child Kathy identified in the preconference as one who might have difficulty.

Nadia: Umm, if we have . . . six blueberries and five . . . strawberries, we will get eleven, but if you take away three strawberries, you'll still have eleven.

Kathy: Hmm, let's try that. If I take away 3 strawberries, how many pieces of fruit are there altogether?

Nadia: One, two, three, four, five, six, seven, eight.

Kathy: Eight. And we need eleven.

Student: That's another way to make an eight?

Kathy: That's a way to make eight, but we're going to make eleven, okay?

Kathy is kind, patient, and thoughtful in her interaction with students. Nadia's statement may indicate that she is not yet conserving number. Kathy is aware that other children may be puzzling about the same idea. She models Nadia's conjecture with manipulatives and assists Nadia in counting the objects. She allows two students to respond to Nadia's conjecture. She also makes a decision to move on, which is appropriate in the situation given that Nadia's conjecture will not bring out important strategies for finding combinations of eleven. Nadia's confusion can be dealt with individually and in small groups. If she is not conserving number she will need lots of counting experiences and discussions before her understanding becomes solid. Teachers must make decisions like this many times every day while they are in the midst of things. This is what makes teaching so challenging and exciting and why knowing both the mathematics and the trajectory of understanding mathematics is important.

Kathy then presents the problem to the students and asks them what fruits they will choose. When she is satisfied that the children understand that they are to choose two fruits, she reiterates the target number, eleven. The children are beginning to get restless and there seems to be an endless number of questions about the task.

Kathy: Okay, and how many are you going to have altogether?

Several Students: Eleven.

Kathy: Eleven. So what you're going to do is take your papers and you can use Unifix cubes if you want, or you can use tiles if they'll help you count . . . shhh . . . And then . . . you're going to somehow—either drawing a picture or using numbers—you're going to show us what kinds of fruit are in your fruit bowl and how many of each. So I might have drawn five blueberries and six strawberries if that was my choice.

Student: I'm going to draw grapes and some apples.

Nadia: I'm going to draw strawberries and oranges.

Student: Could you write them down, too?

Kathy: You can write . . . you can use words, you can use pictures, or you can use numbers. Just so long as you know exactly what fruit was in your bowl. Okay?

Nathaniel: I don't get it. Because, like . . .

Kathy: What's your question, Nathaniel?

Nathaniel: You use some Unifix cubes to make it . . .

Kathy: Yeah, if it would help you.

Nathaniel: And you would have to find out that there's eleven, and then you write it down that there's eleven or draw a picture?

Kathy: Mm-hmm, exactly. Okay? Miranda?

Miranda: Does it have to be eleven?

Kathy: Yes, it has to be eleven. Okay? I see two more hands and then we're gonna go to work. Andrew, what's your question?

Andrew: Are you supposed to, like, make the shape of the fruit that you have?

Kathy: Well, you could draw a picture.

Andrew: No, I mean . . . if you had five and six, would you have to make a picture of it or just make Unifix cubes?

Kathy: Somehow, on this piece of paper, you need to show what your answer is or what you're thinking about, okay?

As I listen to this exchange, I wonder why the authors of the curriculum postponed modeling possible ways of representing the solutions that come up. I also note that Kathy and I were not specific enough about our expectations. The exact wording of the problem could have been written on the board and we could have been explicit about what should be included on the student papers. These are all details we can consider during the postconference. I also wonder if Kathy's concern about being too directive is coming into play.

The students go off to work and Kathy focuses on four children she asks to remain with her in the meeting area. As we agreed, I interact with the students who are not working with Kathy as a way to help her maintain a sense of the whole group. All of the children in the class seem to understand the task and are busily finding solutions to the problem. Most have at least one solution that they are working to represent on paper. Some have more than one solution. Suddenly the period is over and the children go off to science class. Kathy and I collect their papers and ourselves for the postconference.

The Postconference

In Content-Focused Coaching postconferences, the coach initiates and provides feedback on teaching and student learning in terms of specific and concrete lesson content. In doing so, the coach keeps in mind selected core perspectives on lesson design, as represented in the guide. Guided by the general framework of the core issues on lesson design, these highly specific and practical conversations foster dialogue on content and on pedagogical content knowledge.

Because of scheduling issues, our postconference lasts only twenty minutes. I feel rushed and make the classic mistake of trying to squeeze in too much information in too short a time. As a result, it is unclear at the end of the session what Kathy has learned. Fortunately, we will have other times to meet and work together.

I begin the conference by asking Kathy for her reflections on the lesson.

Lucy: So, how do you think it went?

Kathy: It was interesting, because I like working with a small group, but then I didn't get a sense of what was going on in the rest of the class. So it will be kind of interesting to look through these [the students' papers] and try and get a sense of what was happening. So it's something I have to think about. Does it help these four children to have more time one-on-one or in a small group, but then what's happening with the rest of the class?

Lucy: Right.

Kathy: I didn't get to circulate as much as I would have liked to.

Lucy: What about the meeting itself and the way you presented the lesson?

Kathy: I think the point got across, but then when we started working with the actual Unifix cubes I felt like it could've gone on and on. People are noticing really interesting things. They were saying things like, "What if we take away three, what's left?" and I felt a little bit rushed and so I didn't want to get into all that with them. I wanted to send them off and have them try it on their own. I think it definitely was a good idea that I didn't read that story . . . I didn't need one more element. But, I don't know, I'd be curious to see what they came up with.

Kathy is concerned about the trade-off in focusing on a small group of students while the majority of children work independently. This is a new practice for her and it's not surprising that she feels like she lost the sense of what was going on in the rest of the class. From my perspective, it is remarkable that the rest of the class stayed on task and quite engaged without any prompting from Kathy.

Even though Kathy is anxious to look at the students' work, I feel that it is important to talk about her tendency to ask students only to use counting as the way of confirming a sum. This is one specific area that Kathy can easily work on and one that should have a profound impact on the discourse in the classroom.

Lucy: I want to talk a little bit about the language that you're using mathematically so it will help you as you're thinking about this, especially when you go to process it. You said to kids, in the beginning you said, "One, two, three, four strawberries," and then some other child said, "Put four blueberries." And then you counted one, two, three, four, and then you said, "Help me count this." And you got to eight. When you use the phrase "Help me count this," you limit kids to counting as a strategy for figuring out the sum. That's why I jumped in there. There were some kids who said, "It's eight," without any counting. One kid did it on her fingers, but there were three or four voices that called out eight and they saw the double, the four and the four. So, one of the things that you want to avoid saying is, "Help me count this." What you want to say is, "How can we find out what the total is?" That will get you different strategies. One kid will say, "Four and four is eight." Another kid will say whatever they will say. So, avoid the statement, "Help me count this." It keeps kids at the state of counting three times. What I mean by that is, "One, two, three, four"; "One, two, three, four"; "One, two, three, four, five, six, seven, eight." That's counting three times. Okay? For your little ones who don't have one-to-one correspondence, that's where they are so it's not bad to count like that, but let it come from them and you'll start to get more sophisticated strategies.

Kathy: So, asking the question, "How can we figure out how many are here?" some of them may say, "We'll count" and some of them might say, "I just saw it."

Lucy: "I just saw doubles."

Kathy: A lot of them can do that.

Lucy: Yeah, so you don't want to discourage that.

Kathy: Right.

Lucy: Then the little girl says to you, "You need two more strawberries and one more blueberry," and you said, "Will you help me count?" Instead of saying, "How did you get that?" or "How did you know you needed two more strawberries and one more blueberry?" Because that's the math. She answers the question "How many more?" Which is not an easy question for K–1. So she figures three and she splits the three into a two and a one. So that was interesting. The question there could be, "How did you know that?" or "What made you think that?" Do you understand?

Kathy: Yeah.

Lucy: Not "Help me count." You could then get to, "Is it really eleven?" But in her way of thinking about it, she will explain why it's really eleven. You could prove it to your little ones by counting to eleven. Okay?

Kathy: Okay.

Lucy: Then one child said take one out; he made the exchange. He did what's called *compensation*. He did a very big idea in math. He made the compensation. He exchanged one strawberry for one blueberry and kept the total constant. Right? So you said then, "Do you think there's still eleven?" That was a great question. That was a perfect, right-on question. Then you go, "Help me count." The question should be, "Why do think it should still be eleven?" Let the child explain this notion of compensation. Then another kid brings up this notion of *opposite*. What this child is talking about is the *commutative property:* $6 + 5 = 5 + 6$. This is where you have to be careful with language, too, because six strawberries and five blueberries is *not* the same as six blueberries and five strawberries. It is the same total number of fruit.

Kathy: Right.

When I reflect on an exchange like the one above, I wonder about many aspects of the dialogue. We are discussing specific, concrete examples of content and pedagogical content knowledge. This is an important characteristic of Content-Focused Coaching. I am aware that I am doing most of the talking and that I am repeating myself. My intuition and experience is telling me that Kathy is with me and open to this information, even though I am long winded. She is not indicating in any discernible way that she is upset or overwhelmed. My sense is that Kathy has enough awareness of these ideas about early number development that she can hear the difference between the questions and imagine the difference in the discourse. She is building her knowledge of how people learn mathematics and of how teachers can facilitate that learning. She is also a thoughtful, reflective professional who indicates her interest in the nuances of understanding children's thinking. She knows the conversation is about the work. It is not personal and it is not a statement about her worth as a teacher. We both seem to understand that teaching is a "practice," which means that we have to practice it.

I also wonder if I could be doing a better job of checking for Kathy's understanding. By just asking, "Do you understand?" I really have not given her an opportunity to express her understanding. In my desire to assist her, am I giving her too much information at once? Am I trying to pour knowledge into her head? It amazes me when I analyze these dialogues how much my tendency to be the "sage on the stage" emerges even when I consciously want a democratic, respectful dialogue.

We move on to discuss what was going on in the rest of the class while Kathy was working with the small group. I share my observations about the children who were working independently and reassure Kathy that the children were on task and most of them had found at least one solution to the problem. I mention that several of the students worked with the five and six combination, though a number had found other combinations, such as four and seven and nine and two. Kathy tells me what she observed in the small group. This demonstrates that she is a keen observer of her students and wants to know how to use her observations to guide her instruction. This is exciting to me, because I believe that assessment should drive instruction individually and collectively. I make a note to myself to offer in a future coaching session to conduct individual assessments with Kathy of three or four of her most puzzling students. By looking deeply at a few students, we come to understand more about students in general. We also come to recognize the characteristics of different levels of understanding that are revealed as we observe children work on mathematics tasks. Once we better understand students' thinking, we can experiment with ways of helping them move to a deeper level of understanding or proficiency.

Kathy has indicated that she wants to look at the student work and wants to get some suggestions for how to process the work in the next meeting in a way that brings out the mathematics. I turn our attention to the students' work.

Lucy: Okay, so let's look at kids' work. You have to help me, because kindergarten kids' work is not easy for me.

Kathy: Okay. Benny actually had, he had it laid out. He had seven green—and I'm not sure what fruit it was supposed to be—and four red, but then he didn't have time to finish drawing.

Lucy: So he has to finish. Let's put that on the "let's finish" pile, and this looks like another one that isn't finished.

Kathy: Gabriel started with this side and he was doing seven. So he went, four apples and three strawberries. And then he kept on adding one. He added one more and would count the whole thing. He added one more and counted the whole thing. And then when he got to nine total, he just saw it. He said, I need two more to make eleven. And then he started drawing it but he didn't finish.

Lucy: Okay. Why don't we do this relatively quickly? Make a pile of "not finished" and let's go back to only what is finished.

Kathy: This is interesting. I haven't looked at this yet.

Lucy: I think this has three fruits.

Kathy: It looks like she's doing three fruits.

Lucy: So here's a child who's not following both constraints, so we're going to put that one on the side. This one looks done or close enough for us to figure out what they were doing. If this is strawberries and blueberries she counts them to prove it. . . . So we're going to hold on to this one. This one we'll look at. This child has got a bunch going. So, we'll take this. This looks unfinished to me. What would you say?

Kathy: It's either unfinished or it's finished but it's missing.

Lucy: Or it's wrong. Okay. In other words, we're saying that these are not finished for some reason as we look at them. So one of the things you're gonna want to look at is what's on a finished piece of work and begin to establish the standard for a finished piece of work.

Kathy: Mm-hmm.

Kathy and I sort through the children's papers, making piles: a pile of unfinished work; a pile of work that has at least one finished solution; and a couple of papers that show confusion (for example, three addends, or the number seven instead of eleven). We then consider appropriate interventions for each child. As we do this, we begin to get clear about what a finished piece of work might include. This leads us to consider where to start the whole-group conversation with the children.

The fact that at least eight children have five plus six or six plus five as their solution leads us to consider focusing on the commutative property through the idea of opposites. Several children have already used this approach on their papers. A few have other pairs of opposites, such as seven plus four and four plus seven. About half of the students have unfinished papers.

Lucy: One way that you might want to start your meeting is by just looking at combinations that kids came up with, and putting them up, and maybe starting to write the number sentences for them. Establishing what criteria you're looking for in a finished piece of work. So my first meeting would be taking one that you think is finished. . . . Here's a very neat one. Not only has she got the picture, but she's labeled every picture. Okay? And . . . basically she created an algebra sentence here. Five oranges and six lemons equals eleven. Okay? So, five and six, it's the combination that everybody else has been using. And you look at the parts [and say to your students], "Look, she drew a picture. Look, she used letters to label that picture. Look, she drew a number sentence. Let's now look at another one and see what's the same and what's different." Okay? About how they did it. So you take the same combination—five and six—[and ask] "What's the same and what's different?"

Kathy: Mmm . . . That's nice!

Lucy: I used cherries and strawberries, she used lemons and bananas. Okay, that's interesting. What else is the same? We both have pictures, but she kind of used dots, but she showed the real fruit. She labeled her fruit, she didn't label her fruit. But look, she has a number sentence and she labeled this apples and she labeled this strawberries, great. . . . So you want to make sure . . . does your answer have pictures and numbers, and is labeled somehow? Have I used symbols somehow? Okay? So my first meeting is establishing that. Those kids that have finished one [should] think of another one. Okay?

Kathy decides to give the children who have not finished representing their solutions on paper time to do so. She will start tomorrow's lesson by focusing the class on one child's paper that has a solution that includes both a picture and a number sentence. This will help her make explicit to everyone what constitutes a finished piece of work. She will ask those who have papers that show at least one solution to find others. One child has several solutions that are listed in an unorganized way on his paper. This prompts us to think about ways to help him organize his answers in a way that allows him to answer the question, "How will you know if you found them all?"

Kathy: And for someone like—our friend over here—who's thinking of all the combinations he can and not doing pictures?

Lucy: Don't show this right away, you're going to end up here. But pull this kid over and say, "I love what you're doing. Can you think of every single combination you could think of? " And maybe for him you want to help him organize his work.

Kathy: Yeah.

Lucy: Because he'll never see that he has them all. . . . So we're just going to write the numbers here and you can start doing this [listing the combinations] . . . with him. And ultimately he may be the one that gets up and explains this.

Kathy: Okay.

Lucy: You see what I'm saying? But you're going to guide him there by starting with the numbers he's got. And then ask him, "Well, you think some are missing?" You know . . . if he did seven and four, and then eight and three—so he's already thinking in a pattern, all you have to do is get that pattern linear here, so he can see the pattern.

Kathy: Okay. Yeah, that's nice 'cause then at the end, if we do do a chart altogether, he can be . . . checking his work, or—

Lucy: He can be very verbal about it.

Kathy: Yeah . . . okay . . . good.

We have said many things in twenty minutes and Kathy will have to sort through them and decide how to implement the ideas that make sense to her. Both of us wish we could have more time to work out the details, and we both express our gratitude for the collaboration. I am confident that this is the beginning of a productive professional relationship. I take a few minutes to write myself some notes about our encounter and ideas for next steps.

Chapter Six

Coaching an Experienced Teacher: The Case of Dave Younkin

The School

Dave Younkin, like Kathy Sillman, teaches at Public School 234.

The Teacher

Dave Younkin is an experienced teacher who is new to the staff of PS 234 and to grade four. During the eight years before coming to PS 234, he taught kindergarten through third grade in both parochial and public schools. He had not received any professional development in mathematics at his previous schools and was a bit nervous about being videotaped. At the same time, he realized that he learned a lot by talking with and observing his colleagues, and he was excited at the prospect of working in a Content-Focused Coaching setting.

Dave is reflective about his practice and articulate about teaching and learning. His pedagogy is quite refined and he is comfortable with a variety of effective instructional strategies. He has a rich repertoire of pedagogical content knowledge in the areas of social studies and literacy, but he is less confident about mathematics and is not always able to determine the important or "big" ideas he wants to focus a lesson around.

Dave is working with the *Investigations in Number, Data, and Space* curriculum for the first time. His use of the curriculum materials ranges from following the text as written to selecting activities from a unit and sometimes substituting related activities chosen from other sources or from past experience. Learning to work with thoughtfully developed research-based materials like the *Investigations* curriculum presents a new challenge. Dave is an advocate of the approach of mathematics teaching and learning upon which the *Investigations* curriculum was written, but is unsure of the role of prepackaged curriculum materials in lesson planning. The materials are organized in a sequence of units of study. This is similar to the way that Dave preprares his science and social studies curricula. Each unit has a set of activities designed to develop a network of concepts in a given strand of mathematics. Although Dave is comfortable creating such conceptual networks in social studies and literacy, he is less confident about mathematics content. Dave recognizes mathematics as his weakest academic area and is willing to reconsider his hesitancy to use prepackaged curriculum materials.

An inquisitive and reflective learner, Dave took the lead in our coaching sessions. He asked that we focus our work on his questioning and on classroom discourse. I readily agreed to this focus because it would be one way to help Dave articulate the important mathematical ideas embedded in the lessons. I was impressed with both the questions and the discourse that I observed in his class. It occurred to me that many educators would be delighted by the present level of questioning and discourse. Dave's questions were open ended: "What did you notice?" "How can we check that?" They were child-centered and assessment oriented: "How did you figure that out?" "Who can restate what was just said?" Missing were probing mathematical questions designed to bring out the concepts embedded in the activities.

Dave was genuinely curious about his students' thinking, and listened with an open mind. He was aware that sometimes he was listening for a particular predetermined response, and he wanted to learn to listen more consistently with an ear toward understanding student thinking. The students were attentive and practiced in paraphrasing and in asking questions. Yet both Dave and I knew there was room for improvement and were excited by the opportunity to experiment with more probing questions that might deepen the mathematical content of the discourse.

The Class

The culture of Dave's fourth-grade class is one of patience, respect, and caring. All twenty-nine students are expected to take a "we're in this together and here for each other" attitude in their interactions. The class discourse evidences many characteristics of a learning community. Children share their ideas and question each other's thinking.

Sometimes students challenge each other by offering counterexamples. The children are adept at paraphrasing each other's thinking and acknowledging good ideas. There is a range of mathematical understanding among the students. A few students have a superficial understanding of place value and number sense in general. Others are highly articulate and advanced in their mathematical thinking.

Dave employs various kinds of group structures and bases his grouping decisions on the nature of the task. He has developed and implemented several management structures and routines that nurture students' autonomy and awareness of their interdependency. There are four students at each work table. They sometimes work independently, sometimes with partners, and sometimes as teams. Dave's class flows easily from partner work to whole-group discussion to small-group projects. The transitions are quick, orderly, and relaxed. When working in teams, students decide who will get the needed supplies and how to divide the work. The room arrangement is designed to accommodate the easy flow of traffic from desks to whole-group meeting area to supply areas. Supplies are kept in central, neatly labeled locations, and students are responsible for retrieving and returning supplies as needed and for maintaining the meticulous room environment.

Many of the students are highly motivated and often come up with conjectures and questions or take assignments further than required. Some are new to the school and to progressive education. Active participation in lively discussions is a new expectation for these youngsters. Though they are encouraged to dive in and participate in the discussions, Dave works to shelter these students a bit as he nurtures their habits of discourse and their confidence. He struggles with balancing the need for a "safe" environment for the less-skilled students with his desire to have a free dialogue process in which students talk directly to each other, even in large-group settings, without being called on by the teacher.

An environment like this is conducive to focusing on and refining the nuances of teaching important, rigorous mathematics to a wide range of students.

The Lesson

"Combining Fractions in a Design" is a fraction lesson for fourth or fifth grade. It is from the unit "Different Shapes, Equal Pieces" in the *Investigations in Number, Data, and Space* curriculum (Tierney, et al. 1995). The lesson requires the use of Geoboards. Geoboards are square boards on which twenty-five pegs equidistant in placement form a five-by-five array (see Figure 6–1). The pegs form the vertices

Figure 6–1
Geoboard

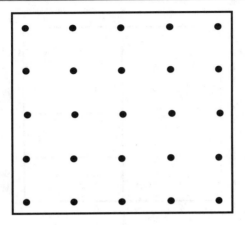

of sixteen smaller squares arranged in four rows and four columns. Students make shapes on the Geoboards by placing rubber bands around a subset of pegs. These boards are used for exploring geometric concepts such as area, perimeter, and the Pythagorean theorem as well as fractions in an area model. The Geoboard designs are often transferred onto Geoboard dot paper with the same five-by-five array. This allows students to make permanent records of particular designs or figures and to write about and compare them.

"Combining Fractions in a Design" requires students to cover the whole area of the Geoboard by creating shapes that make up halves, fourths, and eighths of the Geoboard and combining them into a whole (see Figure 6–2). The rules are similar to those of previous activities:

> There are a few rules about halves that will hold for similar activities in the rest of this unit:
>
> - Each half must be contiguous—that is, it can't have two or more disconnected pieces.
>
> - Each solution must use all the area of the figure. It is against the rules to throw away some of the area and divide what remains into fractional parts. ("Different Shapes, Equal Pieces," 23)

What Is the Mathematics in This Lesson?

This unit of study and this particular activity explore an area model of fractions. The entire Geoboard square is considered the whole or the unit, and each of the sixteen smaller squares is considered to be

Figure 6–2
One design that represents halves, fourths, and eighths on a Geoboard.

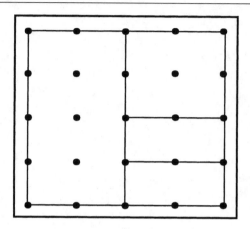

one-sixteenth of the whole. Students divide various regions into smaller shapes (squares, rectangles, triangles) and determine the fractional value of each shape in relation to the entire Geoboard square. They combine various shapes together to create a whole. Students are to label each part of the design with correct fractional notation and then write equations that represent the design. Going from concrete shapes to numerical representations is at the core of this lesson.

On one level, students are working with shapes, squares, rectangles, and triangles. On another, they are working with fractions. For example, if the entire Geoboard has a diagonal constructed from one vertex to the opposite vertex, two congruent right triangles would be formed. We could say that each of the triangles is half of the Geoboard or that the two triangles together make up the whole square. These are statements about the particular shapes. If we consider the area of each of the shapes as a numerical value, we could say that $\frac{1}{2} + \frac{1}{2} = 1$. This statement is about numbers and is more abstract than the statements about the shapes.

This activity is designed to give students experience with the relationships among common fractions. Children are likely to be less intimidated when they need to add a string of fractions: $\frac{1}{4} + \frac{1}{2} + \frac{1}{8} + \frac{2}{16}$. They are likely to develop "fraction sense" in the way that they develop number sense for whole numbers because they are focusing on understanding the relationships. The Geoboard gives students a physical model that allows them to envision fractional parts in various forms and in relation to each other. For example, converting from sixteenths to eighths becomes obvious when working with physical models in which you literally combine two sixteenths to create one eighth or divide one eighth into two sixteenths. There is a proportional relationship between the size of a piece and the size of the denominator when comparing the fractional parts of a whole. It is an inverse relationship; that is, the larger the number of pieces you divide the whole into (represented by the number in the denominator), the smaller the piece. It takes two-fourths of the same referent whole to equal one-half, and the fourths are exactly half the size of the half, or the half is double the size of the fourth.

From exploring these kinds of relationships, it becomes clear that half of a fourth is an eighth, and that that can be represented as $\frac{1}{2} \times \frac{1}{4} = \frac{1}{8}$. By connecting the equation with the action of halving the region on the Geoboard that represents one-quarter, students begin to visualize what it means to multiply fractions. When asked what is one-half of one-fourth or one-fourth of one-half, students can literally see when they carry out the actions on the Geoboard that in both cases the answer is one-eighth. Whereas, when asking how many fourths are in one-half ($\frac{1}{2} \div \frac{1}{4}$) the answer will differ from how many halves there are in one-fourth ($\frac{1}{4} \div \frac{1}{2}$). In the former there are two-fourths in one-half while in the latter there is one-half of one-half in one-fourth. Division of fractions can also thus be modeled and understood by using the Geoboard. Although we want students to have concrete representations for fractions, we don't want them to think that $\frac{1}{16}$ *is* one of the small squares on the Geoboard. Teachers should be aware of the importance of the model in setting the unit value of the pieces (in this case the Geoboard is the whole and the smaller squares are each one-sixteenth of the whole). The numerical values are abstractions and possess properties of their own.

There are many other concepts about fractions embedded in this unit, not all of which can be discussed in one lesson. It is incumbent upon the teacher to decide which concepts will be the focus of discussion. This decision depends on students' expressed ideas and confusions and their questions, as well as on the teacher's knowledge of the structure of the unit, including the focus of subsequent lessons.

Where Does This Lesson Fall in This Unit and Why?

The lesson appears early in the unit, after students have had several experiences working with Geoboards to explore congruent and non-congruent halves, fourths, and eighths. An area model of fractions is explored throughout this unit of study. Students divide squares and rectangles into parts and determine the fractional value of the parts. They combine various fractions to create a whole. They are interpreting fractions as parts of wholes rather than as the result of dividing two numbers or the ratio of two quantities. Students then examine the relationships among specific sets of fractions, such as halves and fourths or fourths and eighths.

Previous lessons in the unit have focused on the concept that comparing the area of the piece to the area of the referent whole is the criterion for determining the size of the piece, and on the idea that pieces with equal areas do not necessarily have the same shape. It is easy for students to see that congruent (same size and shape) pieces are equal in area and therefore will have the same value. It is more difficult to understand that noncongruent pieces (different shapes) can also have the same area (equivalent size) and, therefore, have the same fractional relationship to the referent whole. In "Different Shapes, Equal Pieces," students are challenged to find ways to prove equivalence of area for the noncongruent shapes they create.

History of the Coaching Relationship

Dave and I worked together a few times prior to this meeting and we were developing a good rapport. He often used our coaching sessions as opportunities to ask my opinion regarding concerns he had about teaching mathematics in general, and I sometimes too eagerly took this as an opportunity to provide long explanations of the theories I espouse. When I read the transcript or watch the videotape of this session, I am aware that I do a great deal of the talking. I wonder what Dave actually learns as a result of the sessions and whether my posing questions rather than giving advice would be more fruitful in the long run. There is a tension between these two coaching moves, similar to the tension in teaching. I strive for balance as I experiment with what can be learned effectively from explanations versus what can be learned only through experience and guided reflection. It seems to be my pattern to provide a lot of suggestions and input in the early sessions I have with teachers. There comes a time, however, when the dynamic shifts and I become more of a colleague intrigued with my partner's thinking and marveling at his ingenuity (see the Katherine Casey case study).

Dave and I are still learning to relate comfortably and Dave appears to want to tap my expertise at this stage. He also seems unsure of the mathematics and is receptive to my suggestions and explanations. I continue to wonder how much mathematics can be learned in the planning sessions and how best to encourage people to begin where they are and learn what they can. Even though I am quite active in helping Dave plan the nuances of this lesson, he retains control over which suggestions he will incorporate and what role I will play in his classroom. This is crucial in a coaching relationship. Gently nudging the teacher to take a step or try an idea is balanced with backing off and letting the teacher decide what risks he is ready and willing to take.

The Preconference

Dave starts the preconference session by describing the logistics of the lesson he has in mind. I am familiar with the unit "Different Shapes, Equal Pieces" and have assisted several teachers in implementing it. Even though I am familiar with the unit, I am aware that this session is unique to Dave and his class. Once again I am awed by the dynamic, interdependent nature of lesson planning.

Dave describes related prior experiences the class has had and shares his concern that the students may be challenged by the tasks of combining fourths, halves, and eighths. This concern is a good sign to me, because it signals that Dave is considering prior knowledge and experience in his lesson design, which is one of the core issues of a content-focused perspective (What is the students' prior knowledge? What relevant concepts have already been explored with this class?). It has been my experience that combining fractions physically on the Geoboard is not problematic for students. Filling the board with exactly one-half, one-fourth, and two-eighths might prove challenging for some. On the other hand, students often have trouble combining fractions symbolically and they sometimes have trouble proving that a given shape is an eighth or a fourth or a half.

I am curious about what Dave has in mind. Prompted by his questions, I probe his thinking about the lesson plan.

Dave: I'm not sure about how well they'll do with eighths.

Lucy: Uh-huh . . . because they haven't explored it yet?

Dave: Well they've explored eighths . . . I mean they really basically understand halving and halving and halving will get you eighths. . . . I think they'll . . . you know, that'll be the challenge for them.

Lucy: Do you think it will be a challenge for everyone? Or for a few kids or . . .

Dave: No, for probably ten out of twenty-nine.

Lucy: So a third of your class will be challenged by going from fourths to eighths?

Dave: Well, with combining them. . . . They can make eighths, but combining fourths and eighths and halves . . . there's definitely going to be some confusion . . . but I'm okay with that.

Lucy: What kind of confusion do you anticipate? What do you imagine they'll be confused about?

Dave: I think they'll just be confused with . . . actually, I think that they're so used to this idea that equal fractions have to make up a whole—that all fourths or all eighths have to make up a whole. But that the idea that you can combine those larger and smaller fractions to make a whole will be kind of confusing for some of them. But I think they'll work through it . . . eventually. . . . I'm not sure that we'll get to a conversation at the end, I mean, which is actually a different activity, but . . .

As I listen to Dave speak, it seems that he is really unsure of what the challenge will be in the lesson. He seems to be unclear about the difference between working with the concrete material and the relationships between the shapes and working with the numerical values. The students are combining the shapes physically, which should not pose a problem. They are not yet combining the fractions, which may prove more challenging.

> To provide assistance tuned to the lesson content and adapted to the teacher's students, the coach must know how the teacher thinks about core issues such as students' prior knowledge and anticipated difficulties. In an atmosphere of mutual respect the coach initiates and invites teachers to share their thinking on such issues.

My questions may have helped Dave to see his uncertainty and may also have raised his anxiety level, as evidenced by his change in topic when he jumps to thinking about the end of the lesson. I decide to drop this line of discussion and refocus the conversation on gathering information about the activities the students have previously worked on in this unit. I am trying to help Dave gauge what prior knowledge students will bring to this activity. Dave seems comfortable discussing this. After a short discussion about the possible misconceptions his students may have, I ask how he plans to start today's lesson.

Dave: I'm just gonna . . . ask them to remember the work we've done with fourths, and that that was one way of dividing a whole—a sixteen-unit whole—into equal parts . . . then just saying that there's many other different ways—many other combinations—of fractions that can make a whole. And then saying that . . . for this work today, you're going to need to use halves, fourths, and eighths to make a whole. Other than that, I don't know. I mean, I was trying to think of a way to put it in context.

Lucy: Well, you have a context, a Geoboard.

Dave: Well, I was thinking of a real problem, like . . . making it into a cake and different kids want different pieces . . . but I don't know how to . . .

Lucy: See, I guess for me, because you've already been working with the Geoboard in this way, I just see it as an investigation of a space. So I don't feel strongly that you need a context. I know some people will disagree with me, but I'd rather not have a contrived context. I'd rather stay with this investigation.

It is interesting to me that Dave is considering a context. The idea of embedding mathematics problems into real-world contexts is one that is advocated by the National Council of Teachers of Mathematics (NCTM) (2000) standards and one that many teachers in our district have been exploring. The danger is that we may become dogmatic about it. The purpose of a context is to give students a way into a problem, to help them mathematize their world and to see the applicability of mathematics. Whether or not to create a "story" for a given exploration is an aspect of lesson planning that is important to consider. Dave seems a bit relieved not to have to think up a context for this activity and seems to agree that the Geoboard provides access into the mathematics. I turn the conversation to how he plans to begin the lesson.

Lucy: Will you model one [solution]? Or will you ask the kids to show you one, or what do you think?

Dave: I always wonder about that. On one hand, I want to be comfortable with that disequilibrium that they move through. And then on the other hand, I know that if I model one, they'll take to it very quickly.

Lucy: The notion of disequilibrium is not to withhold information to get people confused. It's more to push a concept . . .

This is an issue that comes up often in coaching sessions. Teachers genuinely want to challenge their students to think, reason, and problem solve. They sometimes have trouble balancing this goal with the goal of giving clear, explicit instructions. One way to work with this tension is to ask students in a whole-group session to come up with one solution to a problem that has many solutions. This provides clarity for the task, yet it does not take the thinking out of the problem. If combining unlike fractions is a new idea, just seeing one possible solution is not necessarily going to make the problem uninteresting. There are many solutions to this problem; for example, discovering that all the solutions will require two-eighths is an idea that will take some exploration. Congruence and notions of symmetry will still come into play, as will comparison of fractions and equivalence.

I know that the desirability of modeling the problem solution is controversial. It is sometimes argued that modeling may take the thinking out of it for some children. I believe, however, that if the problem is rich enough and has several solutions, starting with a model solution may provide entry. If the model is generated collaboratively with students in an introductory whole-class conversation, the teacher is still allowing the students to construct a solution; at the same time this may provide learners who may not initially understand the task with access to the problem. The danger comes when we insist that the model is the only way or the right way, or model in such a way that it does in fact take the thinking out of the problem.

> Coach and teacher discuss the use of specific teaching strategies, such as modeling, in the context of particular lessons. They take into account core issues in lesson planning, including intended learning goals and students' present state of knowing.

I have had many friendly debates about this and continue to explore the notion of when and how much to model. Dave and I discuss this for a while and I again bring the focus to the start of the lesson. It is important to get back to specifics in a coaching session, or you may find that, as you waxed on about general theories, time to plan the details of the lesson at hand has slipped away.

Lucy: So my suggestion would be that you think about modeling it once, like ask them to come up with one solution in your premeeting. "Give me an idea of how to do this." And I would have . . . Do you have an overhead Geoboard?

Dave: Mm-hmm.

Lucy: Use an overhead Geoboard, ask them to explain to you how to . . . solve the problem in one way, and have them use their words and not come up to the Geoboard to do it. See if you can get the language going.

Dave: Okay.

Lucy: Then once they do that, ask them to think about one way to change this so it becomes another solution. And that's probably as far as I would go, and to challenge them to find as many different ways as they can and record it.

Dave: Okay.

Dave and I go on to discuss some of the mathematical issues that might come up. We consider the idea of congruence, flips, and rotations. Dave decided to ask for two solutions to the problem as part of his introduction of the problem. Comparing the two will give him an opportunity to discuss congruence and ways of determining congruence. If a solution matches another solution when it's rotated or flipped, it is congruent.

Dave: I feel fine with that . . . because when I've put that out there with fourths or halves, it did push most of them to just think it through and challenge themselves. Even with the fourths quilt—challenging them to come up with four totally different shapes with the area of four, four fourths that were incongruent—that was a struggle, but it was great. Some of them worked for an hour on one design, so I feel fine with just putting it out there that if you can rotate it and it's the same basic combination, not the same combination, the same design . . . [it is the same solution].

Dave is getting clearer about the mathematics in the lesson, but he is uncertain about what his students may or may not know about the relationships among the fractions they have been exploring. He explains that he was planning to discuss the relationship between halves, fourths, and eighths as a follow-up to this lesson. I am a bit surprised that this has not been an ongoing discussion. Having such a discussion is an opportunity to assess student knowledge in a quick and easy way and would give Dave valuable insight. Dave tells me that he decided to wait because the teacher's guide schedules the discussion for the next lesson. He goes on to say that he has had discussions about the relationships among fractions with individual students as he observed them working, but has not had whole-group discussions on the topic. He confides that he often wonders about which ideas to bring up in whole group. I encourage Dave to start the lesson with such a discussion, even though the teacher's guide suggests waiting. Ongoing conversation about the mathematical ideas embedded in the activities is crucial to facilitating the development of students' understanding. Asking students what they are noticing about fractions as a result of the activities gives both the students and the teacher an opportunity to articulate important ideas and to reveal misconceptions, partial knowledge, and confusions that can guide instructional choices.

In this case we discuss the probability that many of Dave's students will notice that one-fourth is half of one-half and one-eighth is half of one-fourth because of all the prior work he has done with his class on halving and doubling with whole numbers. Assuming these ideas do surface, extending the original problem to include sixteenths, thirty-seconds, and so on would provide a challenge to the appropriate students without changing the underlying mathematical concept.

Dave raises the issue that in this case a fourth is equal to four square units, because the area of the whole is sixteen square units. He wonders if he should raise the idea that a fourth expresses a relationship. I suggest that he hold off on focusing on that idea because the next lessons in the curriculum highlight this concept by changing the size of the whole and, therefore, the size of the parts.

This ongoing conversation also models a pivotal feature of accountable talk, that discussion related to lesson content is valued and is part of the process of learning and understanding mathematics. Dave is open to the idea of starting today's lesson with a discussion. He ponders his use of the curriculum guide. Dave's comments reveal his struggle with implementing a packaged curriculum.

Dave: Well, you know what this tells me is, in my effort to move through these units, and this has always been my fear with subscribing to one curriculum, I sometimes catch myself not—like right now—not thinking like what really makes sense. Despite what's written down here [pointing to the teacher's guide], what makes sense for my class? But then on the other hand, the other day, after a math "Do Now" [Dave is referring to the practice of giving students a short warm-up problem before launching the main lesson], my kids got into this whole discussion of how to find area in a quick way and came up with length times width.

Lucy: The formula! Yeah. That's the idea.

Dave: Yeah, which is great, but it was an hour conversation—that they were totally animated about. They came up with a rule for perimeter and some of them didn't get it probably, most likely, but—so it's hard to know.

Lucy: Well, I think the way that I've come to think about this [pointing to the teacher's guide] is this is my jumping-off point. You say to yourself, okay, this looks interesting, I wonder why they did that. Or I wonder why they didn't do this first. And as you start to ask yourself these questions, knowing who your kids are, knowing what the mathematics is, you then make some adjustments. You can open up the problem or you can narrow the problem. You still have to think about what the mathematics of the work is and what questions you are going to ask the kids and how you are going to present it, because it's only sketched here [the curriculum materials]. This is your starting point . . .

Dave: That's a good way to look at it, your springboard.

Dave then raises pacing issues. He is concerned that if he takes the springboard idea too literally, he would find himself going off on tangents. I suggest that tangential diversions occur when a teacher is unclear about the mathematics embedded in the lesson or when a student comes up with a "big" or interesting idea and the teacher makes a choice to go with it. Sometimes a big idea can be noted and put in a kind of holding pen until an appropriate discussion time. Sometimes the big idea is the teachable moment. These are calls the teacher makes based on his knowledge of the concepts embedded in the present activity and the concepts that will be the focus in activities that come up later in the sequence of activities in the unit.

> To validate their shared view of the intended lesson at the end of a preconference, teacher and coach review the agreed-upon lesson plan.

Next, we sum up our lesson plan and discuss the roles each of us will play. I have found this to be a crucial part of a coaching session. In the early years, I would often have wonderful planning conversations with teachers and leave the session thinking we were in total agreement. When I watched the lesson, I realized that what I thought we had agreed to and what the teacher thought we had agreed to were two different things. I have found that a quick review at the end of the preconference prevents a great deal of miscommunication and serves as a dress rehearsal.

Lucy: I want to make absolutely clear, first of all, who's doing what in this lesson and how I can support you. So, why don't you just maybe tell me exactly what you picture, what questions you're planning to ask or how you want me to help you in some way.

Dave: Well, first, I mean, I'd love for you to pop in if something isn't clear or if I've worded something in a way that's not . . .

Lucy: You're sure you are comfortable with that? Because I felt when we worked last time, it made you a little bit uncomfortable, so I want to make sure that you're okay with that.

Dave: Well. I don't know why . . . [puzzled].

Lucy: I think I threw you a little bit on what you were trying to do with the kids. So I want it to be clear . . .

Dave: Oh. Maybe that was good. [Laughs.] Well, we can do it either way.

Lucy: I'm happy to do it, I just want to make sure you're okay.

Dave: Well, let's try it differently this time then. I'll deliver the lesson . . . I guess if I look to you . . .

Lucy: You can ask me a question.

Dave: Yeah.

Lucy: Okay, so if you ask for something from me, then I jump in, but otherwise I just observe and take notes or whatever.

Dave goes on to explain the running order of the lesson. We tweak a few points, then discuss the work time and a few minor management issues.

Dave: Okay, so then I'll just kind of explain to them again, "You need to include fourths, eighths, and halves." If they've mentioned sixteenths, "You can also use sixteenths or thirty-seconds." And then send them off to do the work, first explaining that "You're going to explore with a partner, individually and use the small grids—the small Geoboard papers. And then check in with me, before you go on to recording it onto the larger paper."

Lucy: [Smiling] Nah.

Dave: That's what the book says [sheepishly].

Lucy: No, because that slows you down and it slows them down. "Check with a neighbor, make sure you got the right answer . . ." [I can make this suggestion because I know that Dave is comfortable with the notion that the classroom is a learning community, and he trusts kids.]

Dave: "Prove it to a neighbor."

Lucy: [Nodding] "Prove it to a neighbor," and go on . . .

Dave: And that would be it . . . for today. Then tomorrow, they would bring this [the Geoboard design on dot paper] to the meeting and we would have a discussion about how to prove some of these equations using the square.

Lucy: Right, and we can walk around while they're working. They're gonna be writing equations and we can push their thinking while they're working.

And then later when we speak, we can think about what questions you want to ask in the meeting tomorrow based on what happened today.

Dave: Okay. Good.

Lucy: Okay. Great.

The preconference lasted a total of twenty-nine minutes.

The Lesson

Dave begins with the class in the meeting area and asks his students to think about "What is the relationship between a half and a fourth, or what is the relationship between a half and an eighth?" He instructs them to "Talk with the person next to you. Get some ideas so we can put some of these on the board." The students enter into lively discussions with each other and Dave circulates among them to get a sense of what they are thinking. After a moment he asks the students to share their thinking. One student explains that there have to be more eighths than fourths on the Geoboard, because eighths are smaller than fourths. Another student adds that there are in fact two eighths for each fourth. A third student establishes that it takes four fourths or eight eighths to equal a whole, and that those two fractions are equal. The next student describes the halving concept that Dave and I spoke about in our preconference.

Ben: A fourth is half of one-half, and an eighth is half of one-fourth, and then a sixteenth is half of an eighth, and then it keeps going on and on—you double the bottom number—I forget what's that's called.

Dave: This number?

Ben: Yeah, like you keep doubling that.

Dave: The denominator.

Ben: Yeah, and it keeps being half of the next number.

Dave: Ben, can we write this down? What's your rule for finding these fractions?

Ben: You split them in half and then you double the denominator. If you split a fraction in half, the denominator will be double . . .

Dave: So I have, a fourth is a half of a half [writing on the board], an eighth is a half of a fourth . . .

Ben: Yeah, and then a sixteenth is a half of an eighth, and then a thirty-second is a half of a sixteenth, and a sixty-fourth is a half of a thirty-second and it goes on and on and on . . . [Dave writes these examples on the board.]

At my suggestion, Dave asks a couple of other students to clarify this idea. It is apparent that one of them is clear and the other is tenuous in her understanding.

Dave gives the students the task for the day: "Today your work is going to be to find combinations of halves, fourths, and eighths, all on the same Geoboard, that will make a whole. Okay? We'll do one together first." As planned, Dave has two different students explain how to create a design that meets the constraints of the task. One of the students takes the design through sixty-fourths. Dave then opens up the problem by giving students the choice of working strictly with halves, fourths, and eighths, or of including sixteenths and so on.

Just before the meeting ends, a student raises her hand:

Abby: I noticed something.

Dave: What did you notice, Abby?

Abby: That it starts at one-eighth and then it goes to one-sixteenth, and . . . eight times two equals sixteen, and then it goes to thirty-two, and sixteen times two equals thirty-two. And then thirty-two times two equals sixty-four.

Dave: Abby, that's a really neat idea, the idea that you're actually doubling by, not two, you're doubling the whole fraction by half. By one over two. And we're going to work more on that.

This was an interesting and important exchange, and I took copious notes. I was not surprised that this child suddenly "noticed something" that the class had discussed earlier at great length. This was one of those moments when a lightbulb goes on for someone and it doesn't matter that that same lightbulb went on for someone else fifteen minutes earlier. This is what it means to "construct your own knowledge." There is no guaranteed direct transmission of understanding and knowledge. No one can transfer knowledge through telling alone. A teacher's telling and explanations can lead a student to think about something, but the student must make sense of it for herself. This student was in the process of making meaning and Dave encouraged her to do so. His response, "Abby, that's a really neat idea," is validating. It is exactly the kind of response that creates a risk-free, high-challenge learning community.

Dave's statement that "you're actually doubling by, not two, you're doubling the whole fraction by half" reveals two things to me. Dave is not simply listening, he is interpreting what the student is saying through his own lens. The student is simply noticing a doubling pattern. Dave wants to explain the mathematics. His explanation is more for his own learning and does not really reflect the student's thinking. Dave and I discuss this as soon as the students leave the meeting area and transition into work time.

Dave: See, you know what? I should have . . . if I'd listened more closely, she *was* just saying that she was multiplying the denominator by two. I thought she was saying that she's multiplying the fraction by two, and so then that's the tricky part to me is like, when do I clear something up like that, because she's not multiplying the fraction by two?

Figure 6–3
One way to represent Abby's discovery
that the denominator is doubling.

Lucy: I don't think the rest of the kids got confused there . . . there was no damage.

Dave: Yeah. No, but it's good to think about because she was just saying, "I'm multiplying it by two," and that's the pattern.

Lucy: Exactly.

Dave and I consider ways to represent what Abby said and how her perception differed from Ben's earlier description of the same idea. We experiment with various ways to write the students' ideas symbolically (see Figure 6–3). Dave and I then circulate among the students.

Dave calls me over to help him work with a student. Nick has made a design on his Geoboard (see Figure 6–4) and Dave wants him to understand that each triangle is one-eighth of the whole. Dave asks Nick to cover the whole Geoboard with triangles. He begins demonstrating what he wants Nick to do by stretching rubber bands over the design that Nick made (see Figure 6–5). Nick seems to get even more

Figure 6–4
Nick's design.

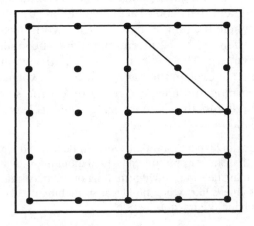

Figure 6–5
Dave asks Nick to cover the whole Geoboard with triangles.

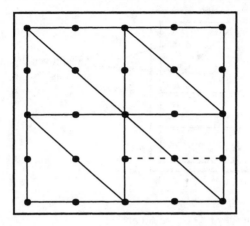

confused. When I join the conversation, Nick has removed all of the added rubber bands and his original design is on the Geoboard (see Figure 6–4). I try a different approach, asking Nick to focus on the parts of the design.

Lucy: Let's start here. If you look at this square [Figure 6–6—bold square below the two triangles] and you divide it in half with the rubber band, would you say that these two shapes, these two rectangles, are equal? [See Figure 6–6.]

Nick: Yes.

Figure 6–6
Lucy focuses Nick's attention on the darkened square and
then on the rectangles within the square.

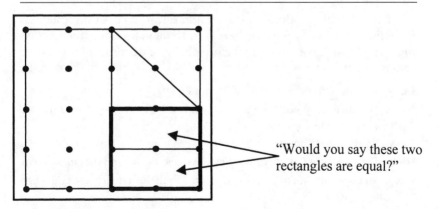

"Would you say these two
rectangles are equal?"

Figure 6–7
Lucy focuses Nick's attention on the two triangles.

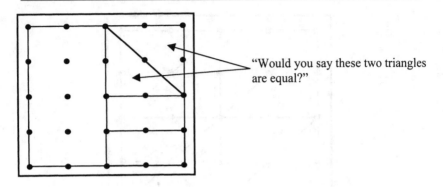

"Would you say these two triangles are equal?"

Lucy: And are they half of the square?

Nick: Yeah.

Lucy: All right, now . . .

Nick: That's a half [referring to the fact that the rectangle (two square units) is half of the square (four square units) and the square is one-fourth of the entire area of the Geoboard (sixteen square units].

Lucy: This is definitely a half. [I direct Nick's attention to the adjacent square above the two rectangles that has been divided into two equal triangles (see Figure 6–7).] Now here, is this a half?

Nick: Yes.

Lucy: Are these two triangles equal?

Nick: Yes.

Lucy: Is this triangle equal to this rectangle [referring to the rectangle below the triangles]?

Nick: No.

These initial questions are closed and result in yes or no responses from the student. My purpose here is to come to a shared understanding of what Nick was thinking before challenging his thinking. I then ask questions that are more open, attempting to probe his reasoning.

Lucy: And how could it be half, if it's not equal?

Nick: Because they both have more than a half . . . one of two halves. Actually, yeah, they both have two.

Lucy: So now you think . . . ?

Nick: They are equal. It's because they have two halves and that makes two.

Lucy: So now you think the triangle *is* equal to the rectangle. And could you prove it?

Figure 6–8

Clarifying the square unit within the triangle.

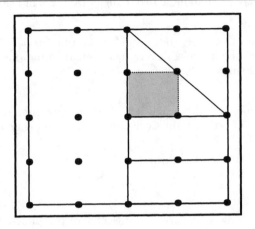

Nick: Yeah . . . say this is a square and . . .

Lucy: Say it's a square. So let's make it a square. [I put a rubber band around one square unit within one of the triangles (see Figure 6–8).] You're saying this is a square, right here? This? [Pointing to the one-unit square within the triangle. Nick nods in affirmation.] Okay.

Nick: Yeah, and these are two halves of the square [pointing to the triangles A and B, Figure 6–9]. And if you put them together, they make one square, so it's equal.

Figure 6–9

D = 1 sq. unit; A, B & C are congruent;
If A + C = D, then B + C = D

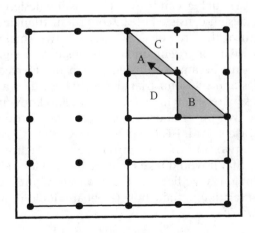

Lucy: Uh-huh, so if I take this triangle [B] and this triangle [C in Figure 6–9] and I move this triangle [B] over here, like this, these two triangles [A and C in Figure 6–9] are equal to these two triangles [A and B in Figure 6–9].

Nick: Yeah.

Lucy: Yes? And therefore, they would make this shape if I put them all together [indicating a two-unit rectangle similar to the one we originally compared the triangle to (see Figures 6–6 and 6–7)]?

Nick: Yeah.

Lucy: Great proof. So now . . . if this is a half [the eight-unit rectangle], what size is this? What fraction of the Geoboard is this [pointing to one of the two-unit rectangles]?

Nick: Hmm . . . it's . . . two [shrugs].

Lucy: Not sure?

Nick: Not sure.

Lucy: Do you know what size of the Geoboard the [four-unit] square is? What fraction of the Geoboard the [four-unit] square is?[Figure 6–6]

Nick: Well, if it's whole, it's a fourth.

Lucy: Okay, so it's one-fourth of the whole Geoboard.

Nick: So it's an eighth [the two-unit rectangle]?

Lucy: So it's an eighth! So what is this [pointing to the two-unit triangle (see Figure 6–7)]?

Nick: An eighth.

Lucy: Very good.

Dave and I take a few minutes to discuss this interaction. We note that Nick was grappling with several concepts at one time and was losing sight of the whole being a sixteen-unit Geoboard. The confusion occurred, in part, because Nick created the triangles Dave asked him to by placing the rubber bands over his existing design (Figure 6–4). The resulting design consisted of six congruent triangles each equaling one-eighth of the area of the Geoboard, two smaller congruent triangles, and two congruent trapezoids, instead of eight congruent triangles and thus became confusing. When he referred to the two-unit rectangles and two-unit triangles as halves, he was considering the four-unit square as a whole. Dave wanted to know if Nick understood that the two-unit triangles were each one-eighth of the whole (sixteen-unit) Geoboard. His intervention was to have Nick cover the Geoboard with two-unit congruent triangles (see Figure 6–5) in order for him to see that it would take eight such triangles to fill the board. Though this might have been a useful way to figure out the size of the triangle in relation to the whole Geoboard, it didn't work for Nick.

Figure 6–10
Nick's correct solution.

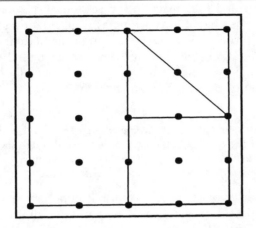

I note that Nick already had a solution on his Geoboard dot paper that showed a half, a fourth, and two eighths as rectangles (see
Figure 6–2). The difference in his new design was that the eighths were
now triangles (see Figure 6–10) and it wasn't clear to Nick that the
triangles were in fact eighths. Nick seemed to be grappling with con-
servation of area. By proving that the triangles and small rectangles
were in fact equal, he could then go on to consider what portion of
the whole Geoboard each triangle represented. Nick appeared to understand the halving concept and concluded that if the triangle and
rectangles were each two units they were each one-eighth of the whole
because they were one-half of one-fourth. As we reflect about our
work with Nick, Dave becomes pensive about listening to children's
thinking.

Lucy: I chose to focus on the shape, because in the past I've noticed that
people, when they shift shapes like that [go from rectangle to triangle], they
lose their sense of area [conservation of area]. So that's where I focused, then
I could go back to other concepts.

Dave: Wow, because I was really looking at it as, he needs to see that this
triangle, that there are eight of these in this larger unit. This whole.

Lucy: That would've been another way to prove it.

Dave: Well, that's what I was trying to have him do, but he got confused.

Lucy: See, but that was your way to prove it, not his way. So what I was
trying to figure out was what was he seeing in those two pictures? It's the
same issue as you were saying with Abby. It's learning to listen so that you're

not trying to give the person a solution so much as you're trying to figure out how they could . . . how you could guide them to their own solution.

What Dave and I discussed in this session in relation to listening and explaining is pivotal in coaching as well. How do coaches listen to colleagues in such a way that we can understand their thinking and the kinds of questions they pursue? How can we help them construct new knowledge by building on their own knowledge? How much modeling, telling, and explanation is helpful?

> For the teacher to learn with the coach during seat and group work, it is helpful for the coach and the teacher to move through the classroom together while collaboratively interacting with students.

I have realized over the years that it is important that the teacher and I travel together around the class during small-group and independent work time. If we are in different corners of the room working with different students, there may be a benefit to more students in the short run, but in the long run the teacher and I do not get the opportunity to learn from each other. A knowledgeable and reflective teacher is going to have an impact on more students over time than the coach was able to help in a given class.

Working together during the individual or small-group time is not always easy or comfortable for people. Sometimes it is best for the teacher to handle the intervention. Sometimes it is best for the coach to do it. Sometimes the coach and the teacher must work with students separately, then come back together. There are no hard-and-fast rules. The goal is to use the opportunity to learn from each other and to puzzle over real concerns as they arise.

The Postconference

"So, Dave, how did it go?" Asking the teacher for his view conveys respect and helps me refrain from making assumptions. I think the lesson went extraordinarily well, and I am curious about Dave's perception. Dave's assessment turns out to be more modest than mine:

Dave: I think it went pretty well. One thing that I was happy with is that I've really been trying to focus on their vocabulary. I wanted to note that and get some feedback from you on that. . . . I was kind of pushing [students to use words like] *vertically, horizontal,* . . . but I don't know if that was clear.

Lucy: I think it's coming along. You also had a child say what the shape was at one point, though at another point you didn't push that. I think that's important, I think you still need to have the words up, like especially *denominator, numerator, fraction, horizontal, vertical, diameter*—those words that are coming up need to be up there so that people could use them in context.

Our postconference dialogue interweaves themes of understanding, probing, and representing student thinking with planning the next day's lesson based on what was learned and observed today. Dave and I continue to reflect on questioning, the use of the blackboard, and teacher interventions designed to nudge a student's thinking to a new level. Dave laments that it is sometimes difficult to know how to intervene. He is sensitive to the range of understanding among his twenty-nine students and to their varying needs, but his understanding of the possible misconceptions or confusions that might come up in relation to certain mathematics concepts is still evolving. I point out that he is now focusing on developing both a deeper understanding of the mathematics he is teaching and the developmental process of learning mathematics. And that's good, because it will enable him to better anticipate what his students' misconceptions might be. Through listening to kids and exploring the mathematics both before the lesson and while interacting with students, he will begin to feel more confident. I remind him that he has created the perfect learning community to allow everyone, including himself, the time and respect to make meaning out of mathematics. Dave goes on to express his surprise at some of the observations his students had about fractions.

Dave: I learned a lot in a way, because I really thought that they—I didn't know that they would be able to make that leap to just kind of defining even a rule of halving fractions so easily.

We reflect on the meeting and note that Dave's opening question and having students talk with partners before the discussion worked well, and that Dave kept the conversation on topic and moving. These were specific concerns that Dave raised in the preconference.

> Providing assistance that is adapted to the teacher requires the coach to make specific suggestions that the teacher finds helpful. The coach's situation-specific and content-specific explanations may help the teacher understand why the specific suggestions are being made, and thus may contribute toward building explicit pedagogical content knowledge.

Dave is also interested in receiving feedback about his use of the blackboard and his choices for representing some of the mathematical ideas and the students' thinking. I remark that he is getting much better at recording student's thinking as it emerges. This takes us to the issue of teacher questioning, which he and I have agreed is important.

Lucy: Now this is going to be nit-picky, but you're interested in questioning so I'm going to push you on this one. . . . Remember when the first child was speaking about how eight-eighths equals four-fourths? And he said that eight-eighths had a lot of pieces and four-fourths has less pieces. He also spoke about the pieces being smaller, that the more pieces you had the smaller they got. "How much smaller?"

Dave: That's a good question.

Lucy: They're exactly half. Because those are the two big ideas—that the pieces are getting smaller, they're actually being halved, and the number of pieces is doubling . . .

We ponder ways of representing the patterns and ideas the students were describing when they talked about the denominators doubling as the areas (the number of pieces) were halving. I suggest that Dave might write the fractions side by side. When the students notice the doubling pattern, he could write "times two" between each denominator of the fractions (see Figure 6–3). One of the students had noticed that the denominators were doubling, but he was not yet thinking about operating on the fractions. Grappling with how to best represent student ideas in ways that are correct in terms of standard mathematical notation is challenging. We want to be careful not to write anything that is incorrect from a mathematical standpoint, yet we want to scaffold the process from the concrete model to the abstract symbols in order to promote understanding. During the class meeting Dave represented Ben's halving pattern in symbols and words (Figure 6–11), which is a few steps away from writing number sentences such as: $\frac{1}{2} \times \frac{1}{4} = \frac{1}{8}$.

We talk about questioning again later in our conference:

Dave: I have one last question. It's about that whole dynamic on the rug of listening to each other, accountable talk, and restating. When I asked Brittany to restate what Ben had told us . . .

Lucy: She basically read it [off the blackboard].

Figure 6–11
Dave's reprensentation of Ben's halving pattern.

$$\frac{1}{4} = \text{half of } \frac{1}{2}$$
$$\frac{1}{8} = \text{half of } \frac{1}{4}$$
$$\frac{1}{16} = \text{half of } \frac{1}{8}$$
$$\frac{1}{32} = \text{half of } \frac{1}{16}$$
$$\frac{1}{64} = \text{half of } \frac{1}{32}$$

Dave: Yes, she basically reads it. What do you do about that? Is that enough?

Lucy: That's where you could push with more specific questions, because I'm not sure she understood it. She could read it, but I'm not sure she knew what it meant.

Dave: When I asked her to explain how Ben did that, she . . .

Lucy: It's not how Ben did that. It's "What does that mean?" See, you don't really care how Ben did it; you care about what does it mean mathematically. If Ben said, "Half of a fourth is an eighth," you could say, "Well what does that mean? What is he saying there?" Or you could ask the question "So, how many eighths is that?" Some way to push at whether or not she understands what that statement means. We know she can read it, we know she heard it. But what does it mean? So the question is more about the mathematics than about who said it.

Dave: That's exactly what I needed to hear. Because I feel like that's what happens, they'll just . . . parrot what somebody else said.

Lucy: Right. And that is where your questioning comes in. That's where you have to start pushing them. So what do you want to push at? That there's two-eighths in one-fourth. That it halved. That it doubled. What's the "it"? The number of parts doubled. The piece itself was cut exactly in half. Those two pieces are equal. The shape of the piece, whether it's a rectangle or a triangle, if it's one-half [of the same whole], they're equal. How can you prove it? Those kinds of questions, those kinds of ideas, are what you're trying to poke at when you get a kid to repeat somebody's idea back.

Dave: [Chuckles] Thanks. That's great, because I've been kind of confused about that. You know—how to get them to talk more about the math, and it's really in how I'm saying it.

Dave and I enjoy the dialogue and he appears to be relaxed and comfortable. I take the opportunity to nudge him about doing the mathematics, the actual activity in the book, before he does it with students.

> The coach explicitly encourages the teacher to build lesson planning habits that include thoroughly thinking through the specific tasks in a lesson and addressing core issues of lesson planning.

Many teachers do not realize the benefits they can derive from doing an activity before they assign it to students. I have often underestimated the level of content; the necessary amount of time; issues regarding materials and setup; and considerations about group size and sharing strategies when I did not do the activity first. By doing the activity, I am often able to predict solution strategies that children might invent and to get a better understanding of the major mathematics concepts that are likely to surface, as well as to determine where in a set of interwoven concepts the particular activity is situated. It is crucial for teachers to make the time to "do the math" as part of the lesson-planning cycle.

Lucy: I'm going to push you on one other thing, and that is to do the activity yourself. If you do it, you will get a better sense of what questions to ask. Because you'll see for yourself what you're struggling with. Because it's not so easy to find noncongruent pieces on a Geoboard. That is not so easy. Or to find a systematic way of finding all the solutions to this problem, or whatever it is. You will come up with a strategy, which will be one of the strategies that they [the students] come up with. So you'll have a sense of what it is that you're going to bump into, especially if you're less comfortable with that mathematics. It's not something you're really solid with. It would be great if you could do it with a colleague. Grady or somebody would do it with you because . . . he may have a different solution or a different way of thinking about it. It would really be nice if you could do that.

Dave: I'll try.

Lucy: I heard you're going to take the math class, right?

Dave: Yes, in August.

Lucy: Great. You have so many pieces in place.

Dave: I feel like that's why I might seem hard on myself. It is because I feel like the management and stuff like that is not an issue. It's just these questions that I hear other people ask their kids . . .

Lucy: It's the content. But you're making a commitment to learn the content and that's all you can do. So figure out ways that you could learn while you're here and what classes you need to take and where you're going to get that support.

Dave: Good. Good plan.

Every staff developer I have worked with has found that this is a big issue for many teachers. When we can engage teachers in doing activities before they try to teach them, the results are quite rewarding. Teachers often do not have (or do not make) the time for this. For some reason, many teachers do not think of doing the activity as part of planning a lesson.

Dave and I then discuss several specific ideas for the next lesson based on what we had learned from this lesson. We agree that the students will continue working independently before a meeting and that they would then be given time to write down statements about what they noticed as well as number sentences to represent the diagrams they created. There will be a meeting in which some of the statements will be shared. Dave will determine this by reading what various students write as they work independently and select the important ideas he wants to focus the meeting on. We both feel satisfied with the plan for the next lesson, and we end the session. The postconference lasted about twenty-five minutes.

Chapter Seven

Coaching a Teacher Leader: The Case of Katherine Casey

The School

Public School 116 is located on the east side of Manhattan, in the midtown area. It is a prekindergarten through fifth grade school serving approximately 850 students from every socioeconomic stratum, race, and ethnicity. More than fifty countries are represented in the student population, and many of the students are second-language learners. The school also serves children who are living in homeless shelters and housing projects. There is a gifted-and-talented program (TAG) in the school. Each grade level has one TAG class and three heterogeneously grouped classes. One remarkable characteristic of the school is that all children are given the opportunity to learn the same mathematics curriculum.

The Teacher

This was Katherine's fourth year as a teacher. She was determined to empower her students with the skills it takes to succeed in school and, ultimately, in life. She knew mathematics well, in some cases better than I. She was eager to learn everything she could about how children learn mathematics and was willing to take the classes and workshops the district provides in order to do so. She welcomed in-class support and her door was open to her colleagues, who often came to observe Katherine's lessons on the days that I worked with her. On the day this lesson was videotaped, there were three people— one teacher, one mathematics staff developer, and one literacy staff developer—visiting from another school in the district. They observed both the pre- and postconference, and two colleagues from PS 116 joined us to observe the lesson.

Katherine was one of the two teacher leaders in District 2's fledgling teacher leader program in 1999. She was instrumental in helping us design the role of a teacher leader. Their tasks involved planning with a colleague, facilitating grade-level meetings and cofacilitating workshops, and continuing to work with a staff developer as they develop pedagogical content knowledge and leaderhip skills. Teacher leaders are classroom teachers who receive extensive professional development in mathematics teaching and learning.

The Class

There were thirty-six students in this heterogeneous fourth-grade class. The class was diverse in every way. Approximately one-third of the children were black, one-fourth were Latino, and one-sixth were children of recent immigrant families, each speaking a different language at home. This was a challenging class. One-fourth of the students had special needs requiring resource room for academics, and seven of the children had significant behavior issues. This was the first class in which Katherine had taken a nonbehaviorist approach to classroom management. She was working hard to build a respectful learning community and was incorporating conflict-mediation skills into her lesson plans. She spent a great deal of time in September and October on building the foundation for accountable talk and socializing intelligence, and continued this work throughout the year.

When this lesson was videotaped in the spring, it was difficult to believe that this was the same group of children, many of whom had extremely difficult home lives, who could barely sit still or talk respectfully when they walked through the door in September. They had been socialized to talk and listen to each other respectfully. They were becoming articulate in expressing their mathematical ideas and they were able to work together in partnerships and small groups.

The Lesson

"More Brownies to Share" is a fraction lesson for third grade from the unit "Fair Shares" in the *Investigations in Number, Data, and Space* curriculum. This is the problem as it appears in the teacher's guide:

> Imagine that you have seven brownies to share equally among four people. About how many brownies do you think each person will

get? Do you think each person will get about one brownie? About two brownies? More than two brownies? See if you can find out exactly how many brownies each person will get. Be sure that each person gets exactly the same share. (Tierney & Berle-Carman 1998, 14)

What Is the Mathematics in This Lesson?

This is basically a division problem (sharing brownies) that results in an answer that involves fractions. Representing division as fractions is a major mathematical idea: "a/b" is another way of writing "a divided by b." Students need help in understanding this meaning of fractions, which doesn't match their usual notions of fractions: that a fraction is an amount, part of a whole, not an operation.

You can consider the group of seven brownies as being made up of seven units or wholes and divide each of the brownies into fourths, or you can consider the group of seven brownies to be the whole and put the brownies into four groups. In the latter case, each of the four groups gets one brownie, then the three remaining brownies must be divided among the four groups. The three remaining brownies may all be divided into quarters, or two brownies may be divided into halves and the third brownie divided into quarters. The lesson involves determining whether each of these strategies yields the same portion and proving that seven-fourths is equivalent to one and three-fourths, which is equivalent to one whole plus one-half plus one-fourth. Children have the most difficulty naming the portion that consists of one whole, one-half, and one-fourth.

Other concepts that are important to this lesson include fractional equivalency, addition of like and unlike fractions, fractional notation, and understanding that parts of a whole may be compared to the referent whole or to other parts of the same whole.

Where Does This Lesson Fall in This Unit and Why?

Katherine's selection of the "Brownies" lesson is an example of flexible use of curriculum materials based on assessment of student understanding. Katherine is aware that the physical model she has been using, Geoboards, appears to be leading some students to the mistaken idea that the unit values of the Geoboards are the meaning of the fractions. Some of her students seem to be developing an idea that half is always eight units because the Geoboard is a total of sixteen square units. Katherine is aware that this is a pitfall of exploring fractional concepts using only one representational model.

When she first became aware of this developing misconception, Katherine took a short detour from the "Different Shapes, Equal Pieces" unit and had her children make fraction kits (Burns 2001, 226).

Students cut strips of paper into fractional pieces and explore the relationships among halves, fourths, eighths, and sixteenths. Each piece is labeled and students then work with their kits in a variety of games and activities designed to help them develop a sense of the relationships between and among the fractions. The children in Katherine's class have used these kits a number of times and seem to be comfortable with the concept of one-half, one-fourth, one-eighth, and one-sixteenth. However, this model is still an area model of fractions, because the children are dividing up one whole.

The class has also been constructing a number line in the form of a rope that runs the length of the room. On the line are pinned the landmark numbers 0, $\frac{1}{2}$, and 1. Whenever a fraction is mentioned for the first time in class, it is hung on the number line at the approximate location of its value. The fraction may be written in more than one form. For example, hanging directly under $\frac{1}{2}$ are $\frac{2}{4}$, 50 percent, .50, and other forms of one-half. To the left of $\frac{1}{2}$ hang $\frac{3}{8}$ and $\frac{1}{4}$; to the right, $\frac{5}{6}$ and $\frac{9}{16}$, and so forth. This number line is under ongoing construction as the children add to and refer to it often.

Katherine wants to move to yet a different model of fractions, fractions as division, to help her students develop a more robust understanding. She has decided to return to the third-grade math unit to explore the brownie problem. The choice to visit a unit from an earlier grade made sense in this instance because the implementation of the *Investigations* curriculum was in its second year of an uneven and voluntary implementation and many children had not had the Fair Shares unit in third grade. Katherine chose the brownie problem because the answer is the result of dividing two numbers: seven brownies divided among four people. The problem is also likely to inspire a conversation about what constitutes the whole. The whole in this case is seven brownies, which introduces the notion that the whole can be more than one. This problem is also likely to make some students think about fractions as ratios. When you think of the answer seven-fourths ($\frac{7}{4}$) as representing seven brownies and four people, you are thinking of the fraction as a ratio of two quantities. This is different from thinking about $\frac{7}{4}$ as the result of dividing two numbers, fraction as quotient (Chapin & Johnson 2000, 75).

History of the Coaching Relationship

I met Katherine about a year and a half before this spring session was videotaped. We had worked together a number of times during the previous school year and every week since September of the current year. We had developed a collegial working relationship that both of us enjoyed immensely.

As a result of our ongoing relationship, Katherine has internalized many of the questions that are inherent to content-focused planning. For example, she regularly considers ways her students might solve a problem, what language they might use to express important ideas, and what confusions or misconceptions might arise. These considerations lead her to create helpful visuals and to pay attention to the phrasing of her questions and explanations. Before our preconference for this lesson, Katherine solved the brownie problem for herself then she solved it in the ways that she expects her students may solve it.

> How the coach and the teacher divide up their roles during the enactment of lessons depends on the history of their work relationship. The goal is a highly interactive and flexible collaboration that allows for coconstruction of lesson plans, mutual assistance during lessons, deliberate experimentation with new ideas, and rigorous collaborative reflection on student learning.

Because Katherine and I have been working together for more than a year, we are often able to coteach a lesson. Katherine is very comfortable with my intervening during a meeting and also asks me to conduct parts of lessons she is unsure of. We seem to be able to toss the ball back and forth with ease. We experiment with new ideas and reflect together in an easy collaborative manner. She appreciates the times that I teach as being opportunities for her to observe her students more closely or to focus on my questions or teaching strategies. In many ways, we have the kind of working rapport that I imagine Content-Focused Coaching fostering among teachers.

Katherine and I know the children well enough and have been working together long enough that we generally interact with different students during the small-group work time, then share our experiences during the postconference. If the relationship were newer, or if Katherine wanted to learn how to probe children's thinking or wanted feedback on her interventions, or if we were interested in a specific issue, we would work side by side when interacting with students in the small-group work time.

The Preconference

This is my weekly session with Katherine. We have been meeting every week all year. I am aware that Katherine will be working on the "Brownies" problem, which I have had experience with. She is taking this problem out of a unit of study that she has not taught. In preparation, she read the salient sections of the unit, including the authors' ideas about what the primary mathematical ideas are and what the teacher might expect the students to do or say. Katherine has prepared the visuals suggested in the guide. She has done a great deal of the lesson planning before we meet. She uses our session to share her ideas and to get feedback about the parts of the plan she is still wondering about, such as the order in which the different solutions should be presented and discussed during the "congress" or "share" meeting at the end of the lesson. In this preconference, the teacher is guiding the coaching session. Katherine is clearly confident and in control of the lesson. We no longer discuss the role I will play because we are comfortable with each other and used to coteaching lessons. The children are comfortable with my participating in their lessons.

This is an unusual preconference because there are three visitors observing: a mathematics staff developer, a literacy staff developer, and a fourth-grade teacher. All three work in District 2. This session illustrates the fact that Content-Focused Coaching can work in a group setting as well as an individual setting. This was an early attempt at working with a group and one in which the visitors were mostly in the observer role. In later group sessions, all teachers took more active roles in contributing to the planning of the lesson.

Katherine begins the preconference by filling us in on what the students have been doing and sharing some observations about her students' confusion about fractions. They are confusing part/part re- lationships with part/whole relationships, which suggests that they are having difficulty keeping the referent whole in mind. Katherine hypothesizes that this is because she has been using the Geoboard pre- dominantly and that if she changes the context students may deepen their understanding. I concur, and assure her that this kind of confusion is typical.

Katherine explains the different solutions to the brownie problem that she came up with and we discuss her concern that the problem may be too easy for some of her students.

Katherine: So this lesson has them sharing seven brownies among four people. And there's a number . . . I came up with three different ways to solve it. And what I liked about the numbers is that it lent them to the idea, like in one of the solutions, I just share out my four wholes and then I have to split into halves and into quarters [see Figure 7–1]. And I liked that they were manipulating the fractions in different ways [referring to all three strategies]. And this is kind of an easy start. And if it is too easy for some of them, I want them to work with sharing four brownies among five people.

Lucy: It may not be too easy, in the sense that they're unusual numbers, so that you are not going to get exactly a half or a third for one thing, and it's a completely different model. It is a ratio model. So kids who are generally thinking about area when they are thinking about fractions don't necessarily

Figure 7–1
Representations of three solutions to the
"More Brownies to Share" problem.

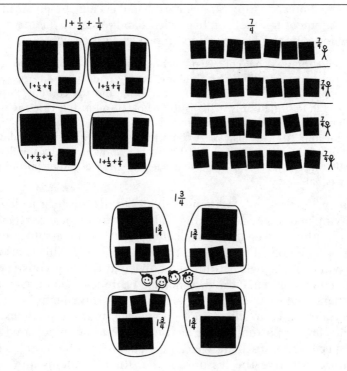

make the leap right away into a ratio [model]. So I wouldn't be surprised if it wasn't so easy for kids—although maybe it will be for some kids.

What strikes me as different about this conversation than conversations I've had with teachers new to this process is that my comments are more speculative. I wonder whether Katherine's top-performing students will in fact solve this problem easily and quickly. I am also aware that Katherine has taken the time to engage with the problem herself and is making decisions based on her interpretation of the difficulty level of the problem and the range of student performance in her class. Even though I am familiar with the children in this class, Katherine works with them every day and has a much deeper sense of each student's level of understanding.

As we examine the various strategies for solving the problem, our discussion intertwines two questions: "What is the mathematics in the lesson?" and "What are our expectations for student work?" Katherine suggests that requiring the students to label the portion that each person will get is challenging and will help us assess their thinking. I agree that naming the portion is one challenge, and add that proving that all three solutions are equivalent would be a second challenge. Katherine shares the three strategies she predicts her students will use. I take a moment to reflect on her process and to clarify the math content by focusing the conversation on pedagogical choices.

Lucy: I like the way that you are predicting what they're going to do. That's really important. And then also thinking ahead about what are the crucial questions that you have to ask in order to bring out the content. So what you're trying to bring out is, what is the whole? And in this case the whole is seven brownies. And then there are other concepts here. What is the name of the portion? And in this case it could have several names depending on how you dish it out. And then the third part is, how do you know they're equal? Is there a way of proving that each of these different portions are actually equal?

Analyzing a lesson's tasks and activities to rigorously articulate the underlying mathematical thinking and the mathematical concepts involved continues to be the most challenging aspect of lesson planning for all of us involved in Content-Focused Coaching. This is also the place where pedagogical content knowledge is being constructed. Fundamental mathematical ideas need to be understood in relation to tasks that make them accessible to students. It is through the lens of the learners, based on their prior knowledge, that the mathematical demands and opportunities for learning have to be understood. The more specific and articulate we can get about this, the more focused and more effective the lesson will be. Rich problems and other materials have lots of mathematical notions and connections; a teacher can easily get sidetracked from the core of the lesson. Katherine and I make a number of attempts at specifically naming the mathematics in this lesson during this preconference.

We then consider whether or not to offer a second, more challenging problem to the students who find this one easy. Katherine likes the one suggested in the curriculum guide, which involves sharing four brownies among five people. We agree that this would be a suitable choice.

Katherine and I invite the visitors to feel free to interact with individual students during the work time, then we continue to work on the details of the lesson.

The conversation moves to Katherine's expectations and management of the lesson. She describes how she plans to begin and the grouping structure she will use:

Katherine: My intro is going to be really short. I'm just going to build the context. I drew the little picture of the four people [see Figure 7–2]. I'm going

Figure 7–2
Visual for the "More Brownies to Share" problem.

to say, "This is our problem that we're going to try to figure out"—not a whole lot of buildup. "All your materials are on your tables. Choose partners from your tables and get going."

Lucy: So they're just going to pick a partner from their table.

Katherine: Mm-hmm.

Lucy: And I think you're right in making it partner work and not group work, because there's only enough work here for two people to be thinking about . . .

Katherine: Right.

Determining the proper group size is important in planning a lesson. For a while as cooperative learning came into vogue, it was the rage to have everyone working in groups of four. However, many problems are better solved collaboratively in partnerships or sometimes triads. It is a valid option to have students work individually, especially when teachers want to understand a child's thinking. Whole-group instruction often begins and ends our lessons. Katherine's class is used to working in all of these grouping structures.

We then consider the opening of the lesson and discuss some of the specific questions Katherine should ask during the preliminary group meeting to help guide the students' thinking.

Lucy: You could ask things like, "Do you think you are going to have more than a whole brownie or less than a whole brownie?"

Katherine: It's here [referring to the teacher's guide]. "How many brownies do you think each person will get? Do you think each person will get about one brownie? About two brownies? More than two brownies? See if you can find out exactly how many brownies or how much brownie each person will get."

Lucy: I think it is worth asking a couple of these questions before they start, definitely. Just watch the time.

Katherine: Okay.

Next, Katherine poses some questions about the "math congress" that is to be held after all of the students have worked with a partner on the problem. We consider the complexity level of each of the solutions and decide that we will start the meeting by selecting students who solved the problem by dividing every brownie into four pieces and then dealing them out. We choose that solution because in our work with Cathy Fosnot's Mathematics in the City Project (Fosnot & Dolk 2001b) we have come to believe that it is best to work from the most accessible strategy to the most complex.

This aspect of lesson planning has proven to be very important. I used to begin the congress with very open-ended questions, such as, "What did you notice?" or "Who wants to share?" and then chose someone to begin. I began to understand that this left too much to chance. If teachers want to guide children in their construction of important mathematical ideas, they have to orchestrate the conversations to some degree in order to focus attention on those ideas. The teachers I work with now take notes about children's strategies when they are working in small groups or partnerships. In our lesson planning we give thought to which strategy is likely to be the most accessible for the greatest number of students. We then identify the children who used that strategy and ask one of them to begin the discussion by sharing their work. We cannot always control what strategies will follow, but we usually consider an order that we think makes sense. We then compare strategies and consider questions of efficiency. It is not always easy to decide where to begin a meeting, but the practice of discussing where to begin and articulating the reasoning informing our choice has been extremely beneficial in creating effective lessons that result in deeper student understanding.

After we decide which solution we will explore first, Katherine asks about whether she should write on the board the addition number sentence that represents adding one-fourth seven times.

Lucy: First of all, I would see if a child came up with that idea. In other words, does a child say, "Well, look, we could add one-fourth plus one-fourth plus one-fourth plus one-fourth plus one-fourth plus one-fourth plus one-fourth and that's seven-fourths." If not, toward the end of the conversation, you might make a string of one-fourths and say, "How would you add these up?"

"What would you call these things?" And then see if you could push for that kind of thinking coming from the child, rather than to demonstrate it. If you don't get it from the children, then demonstrate it. I wouldn't hedge from demonstrating, but push first for that and see if you get it and then notice, for example, that the seven is greater than the four. You might ask a question like, "Well, what do you notice about this fraction?" "Does this look like any other fraction you've seen before?" "What's different about it?" "What's the same about it?" And see if somebody notices that the numerator is greater than the denominator. "Well, do you think it's more than a whole?"

Katherine: Well, in the congress, should I be focusing on getting the different ways up or going deeply on one way?

Lucy: I would build many ways. So first I would want to get all three ways up . . .

> Based on a clear understanding of the mathematical content of the lesson and other core issues of lesson planning, such as students' prior knowledge and anticipated difficulties, the coach and the teacher think through different likely trajectories of student learning and how they can be assisted in the lesson.

Katherine has raised an important question, and the answer should relate to the notion of what the core of the lesson is. The strategy I suggest seems like the best one to use to bring out the notion of fractions as division. But Katherine expresses concern that she will not be able to tie up all the loose ends by the end of the meeting.

Katherine: So that's a chunk of time.

Lucy: Yeah.

Katherine: If I'm going to have kids repeat back and say, "I understand it" or "What did she say?" "Can you put it in your own words?"—that in and of itself takes about ten to twelve minutes, four minutes a group.

Lucy: But I think it's worth it.

Katherine: I think it's definitely worth it. We may just get those three [solutions] up and have the class responsible for understanding that there are three different ways and these are the ways that work, and then get into the math on a different day.

Lucy: And that's okay . . . you know these conversations can go over two or three days.

Katherine: Right. Good. It's not going to happen by 10:15.

Lucy: Sure, and I wouldn't worry about that. Because this is the first in a string of these kind of problems for one thing . . . and, for another thing, what's the point of going really fast? Then nobody got anything out of it.

Katherine: Exactly! Just making sure.

The major anxiety many teachers still grapple with is the felt need to cover the curriculum. In our testing-frenzied environment, this anxiety seems to grow exponentially with each grade level. I often find myself having to reassure teachers that learning takes time, experience, conversation, and repetition. Children are not robots and learning is not linear. Every child learns something different from a lesson. Breaking out of the factory model mind-set of schooling is an ongoing challenge for all teachers and coaches.

The preconference lasted twenty-one minutes.

The Lesson

Katherine begins the lesson as planned. She displays the drawing she prepared, presents the problem succinctly, and asks the students to estimate the portion that one person would get when four people share seven brownies. Students share a range of initial estimates and some explain their thinking. Katherine makes explicit her expectations for the finished product, emphasizing the need to label, using fractions, the portion that each person gets. She keeps the opening meeting contained to five minutes. In that time she answers all the questions the students raise regarding logistics, and reassures a student who is concerned about making a mistake.

Student: What if you get the wrong number of brownies?

Katherine: Then you fix it. . . . I mean, the whole point is for us to learn how to do it. So if you make a mistake, then your classmates will help you figure it out . . .

This interaction is worth noting because it is an example of socializing intelligence. Katherine makes explicit the values and expectations of a learning community, making it more likely that her students will take intellectual risks, expose their confusions, and ask questions when they do not understand.

During the work time, Katherine and I circulate among the students and notice that the three solutions we expected are indeed the ones the students use. Where we notice confusion, we intervene with questions designed to provoke reasoning.

Two children with whom I work solve the problem by sharing one whole brownie, one half brownie and one quarter brownie, then grapple with what to call the total portion. When I question them it becomes apparent that they are not thinking about fractions as expressing a part/whole relationship. They are thinking of one-fourth as a given quantity, as if all one-fourths are the same. At one point they take out their fraction kit and try to compare one-fourth of the brownie with the one-fourth in the kit. The whole brownie is about an eighth of the size of the whole in the fraction kit. I point out to the children that they really can't compare the pieces representing one-fourth of a brownie with the pieces representing one-fourth in the fraction kit because the wholes are different sizes.

I continue to work with these students for a few more moments. They are in a state of disequilibrium as evidenced by their confused looks and their awareness that something about their thinking is not quite right. They will have many opportunities to puzzle through this. This is an example of a time when "telling" does not guarantee that students will understand what they are told. The idea that fractions represent relationships to a given whole is one that students have to grapple with for themselves, argue about, and experience more than once in several different contexts before they have a solid understanding. The very interesting conversation that the students and I have illustrates to me that teachers must be open to different interpretations, that our assumptions about how much and what students understand may need to be examined, and that we must be prepared to go where we have not planned to go.

Katherine works with two students who also solve the problem by sharing a whole brownie, a half, and a quarter. She challenges them to think about "How much is that altogether?" When she later checks in with these two girls about what to call the portion, they surprise her with the answer 1.75. They related the pieces to parts of a dollar, thinking about quarters, and named the portion 1.75. They referred to the fraction, decimal, and percent number line that the class is constructing, which is always visible in the room. On it hangs a tag with the fraction $\frac{3}{4}$ and below that, 0.75.

In these two interventions, Katherine and I responded differently even though both sets of students were grappling with the same concept. Katherine chose to ask a provocative question, while I chose to point out a flaw in reasoning. Both interventions are valid. Katherine and I can discuss these interactions during the postconference. Both of us are confident that Katherine is skilled enough to intervene in useful ways when appropriate.

Another child divides eight brownies among the four people. When he discovers his error he goes on to find the whole, half, quarter solution to the problem. This solution is quite common among the students. A number of children divide all of the brownies into fourths; two children try to determine how many fourths each person gets. Katherine selects this pair of girls to start the discussion for the congress. The congress proves to be quite challenging and does not go as predicted.

Student: We thought that it would be easier if we split each brownie into a fourth. Because if we split all of the seven brownies by whole, then everyone would have two brownies, and the person number four would only have one. So we split them in fourths, and we decided that the answer would be each person would have one brownie and three fourths.

The girls surprise both Katherine and me by telling the class that the final solution is one and three-fourths—we were expecting them to say seven-fourths. Between the time Katherine talked with them and the time the meeting began, they must have realized that each person gets seven-fourths, then reduced the improper fraction to a mixed number. The best-laid plans rarely play out as expected, so Katherine simply focused the class on the process that the students used to arrive at their answer in order to bring out the notion of adding like fractions:

Katherine: Okay, so what was . . . their strategy for solving it? Who could repeat back what they did to go about solving this problem? Austin, in a really strong voice please.

Austin: They split all the brownies into the one-fourth because they thought it would be easier. So each person got the same amount.

Katherine: How much did each person get? [Austin thinks.] Chastity, do you want to help him out?

Chastity: Well, they said that it would be easier to split them into fourths, and all together they got one brownie and three fourths.

This excerpt is a good illustration of one of the techniques that we have found helps develop accountable talk. Katherine asks the students to paraphrase in order to determine whether there is shared understanding and to help them develop good communication skills. She then guides the conversation to the aspect of the mathematics that she wants to make salient.

Katherine: Okay. So are you saying that you took each brownie—like this was one of your brownies [drawing a brownie divided into fourths on the blackboard] and you split this into quarters?

Student: Yeah. And we labeled each person, like this is for person number one, so we would write under it this is for person number one, this is for person number two, and person number three and person number four [see Figure 7–3].

Katherine: Okay, so if they did that, they split all seven brownies into little quarters, how many little quarters went to each person is the question.

After a couple of students confirm that each person would get seven pieces, or seven-fourths, Katherine turns the discussion to how to write the fraction. She asks, "How would I write that fraction, seven-quarters?"

The children give three answers—1.75, $1\frac{3}{4}$, and $\frac{7}{4}$—and records them on the blackboard. As is wont to happen, one child begins to

Figure 7–3
The solution strategy presented in the meeting.
Sharing one brownie among four people.

$\frac{1}{4}$	$\frac{1}{4}$	$\frac{1}{4}$	$\frac{1}{4}$
Person #1	Person #2	Person #3	Person #4

explain how to add like fractions. This is an important idea, and I want to clarify it before we go on with the lesson. I ask the student to explain what she means. The result is a rich, revealing, and unplanned conversation about the meaning of the denominator and why you don't add the "bottom" number when adding a string of like fractions:

Katherine: Someone else. Yes, Lisa.

Lisa: I think Leila is right because . . . I know that on the bottom where the four is it always stays the same, but on the top it changes. Since there is seven of the ones, that equals seven, and since the bottom number stays the same, it would be seven over four.

Katherine: Does that make sense, that there are seven of these little fragments that are fourths? Yeah, and that's how you would write it. Seven over four means that you take seven of those quarters.

Lucy: I think Lisa said something very important. Say again, Lisa, what you were saying about how you added up those fractions. Why didn't the four change?

Lisa: Well . . . on the bottom, the four always stays the same throughout any problem, but on the top it changes.

Katherine: Do you know why the four stays the same on the bottom? What that four stands for? Or the bottom number in the fraction? Do you know, Rebecca?

Rebecca: The four stays the same because it's like the fraction one-fourth; it's a quarter.

Katherine: Mm-hmm.

Rebecca: So you can change the one, because it was only one-quarter, but then if you added more, you would have to change the top number, and not the bottom number.

Katherine: 'Cause the four on the bottom says that's the quarter and the top tells you . . .

Rebecca: How many there are.

Katherine: Wow! What do you think, Pemma?

This excerpt provides an example of when a coach might step into the conversation during the lesson. It also exemplifies the ease with which Katherine and I have learned to coteach a lesson.

> Based on a well-established collaboration of coteaching, the coach may even jump in and participate in classroom discourse led by the teacher. The coach supports the teacher and fosters the quality of accountable talk by helping students explain their ways of thinking and helping them focus on the connections that are at the core of the mathematical concepts in the lesson.

We continue to talk about the meaning of the numerator and the denominator. Many students make comments, but I notice one child who looks like he might not be following the dialogue.

Lucy: [To a student] Are you following this conversation? Can you say what you think we're saying?

Student: You're trying to say that when Ms. Casey wrote up on the board the quarter seven times, so you add all the ones on top and it'll make seven, then you just leave the fours alone, and it'll be seven-fourths.

Lucy: Now why are we leaving the four alone?

Student: You leave the four alone because whenever you add, you do the top. Just the top only.

Lucy: How come?

Student: Because [pauses] that's the way the people made it?

[Laughter.]

Lucy: Do you have a reason for why we're leaving the . . .

Student Two: Because when you add the top it equaled seven, but you have to leave the bottom the same.

Lucy: Why?

We are beginning to probe the students' thinking, and the fragility of their understanding is surfacing. The conversation continues for several more minutes. Toward the end, some students are beginning to be able to articulate their understanding.

Rebecca: I agree with him . . . but I disagree with Ron because if it was just four parts, you could cut one really small and one really big. Like, of the brownie, so . . .

Lucy: So what you're saying about the bottom number, the four, is that all the parts are the same?

Rebecca: Same, yeah.

Lucy: And what Steven is saying is, you're counting up same parts. You're always counting up fourths in this case, so all those parts are the same. Did you want to add to the conversation?

Student Three: Yes. I agree with what Steve said, because if you change the four, that means that you're not trying to make it for four people. If you changed it to five, that means you're trying to split it into five things . . . I think the four is standing for the four people, because you're trying to cut the brownies for four people.

The excitement in the air is palpable as the students grapple with these concepts. We are experiencing academic rigor in a thinking curriculum and using accountable talk to develop student thinking. I make one last move aimed at getting some of the students to make a generalization. I am now acting as both coach and teacher. I want to demonstrate this pedagogical move to Katherine so she can add it to her repertoire. I also want to nudge those students who are ready to leap from a specific example to a general concept—namely, that the denominator can be thought of as the number of people and the numerator as the number of brownies. Though this is not the main focus of the lesson, it is an important idea about fractions—and it was generated by the students.

Lucy: So if I wanted to share seven brownies among five people, what would the denominator be? What if I wanted to share . . . maybe I had seven brownies and a friend joined us. And I wanted to share among five people. What would the bottom number be? Any idea? Go ahead.

Lisa: I think it would be five, because you have five friends and you wanted to share with them, so the question is that you have five friends and the answer is, you have to find that out.

The Postconference

We are all eager to discuss the lesson, visitors included. It went well even though the discussion at the end was not the one we planned for. The visitors interacted with the children during the lesson, and they also have ideas to contribute to the postconference. We spend a good part of the postconference sharing our experiences with individual students. This allows us to reflect on evidence of student learning as we consider our next steps.

Katherine begins the session by sharing her exchange with the two girls who decided that the portion of brownie each person received would be 1.75.

Katherine: "You have a half and you have a quarter, is there another way that you might be able to say that?" And I left and I came back and they said, "Well a half and a quarter, that's like money. I looked on the number line . . . a half and a quarter, that makes seventy-five cents."

Visiting Teacher: So you had mentioned half and quarter?

Katherine: Yeah, as just benchmark, landmark numbers . . . So she came up, and she's exactly right, this is 1.75

Visiting Teacher: Yeah, that was good.

Katherine and I then share some examples of children who had trouble naming the portion that was created by combining one whole, one-half, and one-fourth. I had had an interaction with two children, one of whom was confused about what to call each part and the combined portion. This child often struggles to make sense of mathematics and Katherine and I continue to grapple with ways to help her. In this instance, her student partner was able to help her. He explained that the fractional parts in the brownie problem are like quarters in a dollar—each fourth of the brownie is like one quarter of a dollar. This analogy gave his partner entry into the problem, and she was able to name the portion—1.75. This example gives me the opportunity to make a connection to pedagogy.

Lucy: So this business of going back and forth between writing it as $\frac{3}{4}$, or seeing it as 0.75 is not such a hard leap for kids. It's a question of us being comfortable with letting them know that these are different ways of thinking about something, and there are different ways of writing those ideas, but that 0.75 means the same as three-fourths in some cases. You know, so that part that you did here [referring to what Katherine wrote on the blackboard: $1.75, 1\frac{3}{4}, \frac{7}{4}$], although I wouldn't have put the dollar sign up, because it's not really dollars you're talking about . . . that was good that you did that.

My intention here is to make generalizations about teaching and learning from specific examples. I want the teacher I'm coaching to walk away from the session having learned something that is applicable to more than just one lesson.

> Teacher and coach collaboratively reflect on evidence of students' thinking and learning during the lessons coached. In analyzing different learning trajectories and student difficulties, the goal is not only to assess how successful the particular lesson was, but, more generally, to learn about pedagogical content knowledge: What are the students' specific challenges when learning particular mathematical content, and which teaching moves allow us to assist student learning in these areas?

Next we analyze the detour that I took when I asked Lisa to explain why the denominator remains the same when adding like fractions.

Lucy: When Lisa said, "I add one fourth and one fourth and one fourth. The numerators I'm adding, but the denominators stay the same." That's the kind of thing you have to listen for. Because that comment is what's going to push the development of the thinking about fractions. So, I know it took us a little bit off where we were heading, but it was a big idea. Now what's going to happen tomorrow is, you are going to have different denominators. You're going to have a half and a fourth. The denominator doesn't stay the same in that case.

Katherine: But we've investigated that to some degree, so what I'm going to be curious about is, if anyone tries to add the half and the quarter, 'cause they pretty quickly said you can't. This isn't a sixth . . . Because there was one question someone asked, "Well, why isn't that a sixth?" And someone [said], "'Cause look, it's a half and then a quarter, that's huge. A sixth would be tiny." So some of them have started talking about how the fraction has to be the same if you want to group them . . . [Katherine is describing the common mistake of adding the denominators and wondering if any of her children will make that error.]

We continue to consider how students might come to understand that one plus three fourths is equal to one plus one half plus one fourth, and that four fourths equals one whole.

Katherine: I mean, wouldn't someone say, "Well, let's try to put out all fourths and see that the whole has the four fourths?"

One of our visiting colleagues confirms Katherine's speculation by sharing that she witnessed a couple of students doing exactly that. They took fourths, laid them on top of the one half and one fourth, and realized it was three fourths.

We have been discussing our interactions with individual students and considering what mathematics still need tending. Time is short and I want to make sure that the conversation addresses Katherine's questions and concerns before we end.

Lucy: Did you want to speak about anything in particular?

Katherine: No. As usual, it's just whenever there is a math congress, it's which part do I now focus on? And I think you jumping in and focusing on the numerator–denominator was an important relationship for them to get. I always imagine, well, what if Lucy weren't here, where would it have gone? [Laughs.]

Lucy: Well, what would have happened is that you probably would have gotten to the next solution and that other conversation would have come out somewhere else along the line. It's not like it had to happen there, but you have to listen, when kids are talking, for those pieces that are going to get you that kind of conversation.

Listening to students with an ear toward hearing them try to articulate important and relevant concepts is very challenging for most of us. Katherine wrote the number sentence $\frac{1}{4} + \frac{1}{4} + \frac{1}{4} + \frac{1}{4} + \frac{1}{4} + \frac{1}{4} + \frac{1}{4}$ on the blackboard and posed the question "How would you write that fraction?" Lisa described a procedure that involves adding only the numerator and keeping the denominator constant. Many children learn this procedure, but don't understand it. It is a procedure that only works for like fractions. When there are unlike fractions, children make the mistake of adding both the numerators and the denominators. Though we had not predicted that this concept might surface, it did. I chose to go with it because I thought it might bring out the meaning of the numerator and the denominator in this problem. I was aware that some of the children used language like "seven out of four." That language is less appropriate for this problem. The seven represents brownies and the four represents the number of people the brownies are to be divided among. Katherine had strong content knowledge and a deepening understanding of how children learn mathematics and what possible confusions or misconceptions may arise. My goal was to help her begin to identify the teachable moments.

In the following exchange, I try to take the more general idea of "teachable moment" to the specific.

Lucy: And Lisa . . . she is this close to making a real generalization about people and brownies, right? I changed the denominator on her, and she almost got that it would be seven over five, but then she said, "You have to figure it out." So, if you gave her two more problems, this kid would have that generalization.

Making generalizations is what gives us power mathematically. Going from the general to the specific or from the specific to the general are two paths that are aimed at making connections. Making connections develops the conceptual network of ideas that allows us to apply what we are learning in new situations.

A little while later in the conversation we return to the question "Where will you go next?"

Lucy: So I think you started at the right place [starting the congress by focusing on the solution seven-fourths]. What do you think, and where will you go next?

Katherine: I will definitely go to the next solution [$1\frac{3}{4}$], which I think will bring up the idea of numerators and denominators again, and proving are these the same [$\frac{7}{4}$ and $1\frac{3}{4}$], are these different? Here's the whole. How does that work? There's a lot of conversation that can come out of this, and different combinations of numbers as well. Once they start getting big ideas about the number of people versus the number of pieces . . . the numerator–denominator relationship, to test that with different configurations of sharing . . . will deepen that . . . let's test those big ideas. And then another one—we haven't even come to the idea of, seven-fourths of *what*? Like, what's our whole? So, you have one and three-quarters out of what? You know what that is? That's seven brownies.

Lucy: That's tough. That's going to be interesting.

We are grappling with the notion of the whole being more than one. In retrospect, for this task you wouldn't ask, "Seven-fourths of what?" Rather, you'd ask, "One-fourth of what?" The response would be seven, which represents the whole.

Next we reflect on what transpired during the congress. I point out that the two children who shared their solution stated the answer as one and three-fourths. Yet most of the meeting revolved around their strategy, which involved dividing the seven brownies into fourths. I agree with Katherine's suggestion to begin tomorrow's lesson by asking students to consider the solution one and three-fourths. She might ask students to compare seven-fourths and one and three-fourths, with the aim of proving equivalency, then bring in the third solution (one, one-half, and one-fourth) and prove equivalency among all three solutions.

Before the postconference ends, I reflect with Katherine from a larger perspective.

Lucy: You know, Katherine, I have to comment on how far the class has come.

Katherine: Oh, that's good.

Lucy: And when we think about where they were . . . If you saw this class in September, they could barely add. Conversation was not something they were good at. Listening to each other was a miracle. They have come an enormous way. And the techniques of having each child listen and respond back is just ingrained in the class now. They even respond to each other—if you listen to the language that the children are using—"I disagree with this one." "I support this idea." That is an amazing accomplishment, and I think you should feel really good about that.

Katherine: They sounded really great, and I get to have them for another year.

Visiting Staff Developer: It is a spectacular accomplishment . . .

Lucy: And the way that they're making connections between and among the different things that you're doing is another good sign, because it shows that you have really taught them that it's all about thinking about things. It's all about making connections about things. And that's what good learning, especially in mathematics, is all about. Because most of us learned mathematics in isolation we didn't see how it was connected to anything. We had no application for it, and we're not very good mathematicians as a result of it. But these children are breaking that mold and that's great. It's very exciting.

One of the guiding principles of Content-Focused Coaching is that teacher and coach learn from each other. We arrange for visits from other teachers in order to give teachers an opportunity to learn from each other. I want our visitors to have the opportunity to give us feedback and to reflect on their own learning.

Lucy: [To visiting teachers] Did you want to say anything?

Visiting Teacher: I enjoyed hearing them talk about it and working it out with each other. And, just as you said, listening—the way they listen to each other. That is a wonderful skill that most of us have not been able to develop in our own children. And they are willing to share and do . . . And the way they thought it all through is very clear, and they accepted each other's solutions and they didn't say, "Oh you're wrong" as you often hear.

Lucy: And she actually set that up in the meeting again, I'm sure it's been [set up] many times. When the little boy asked, "What if I get the wrong answer?" or whatever his question was, you said, "So you'll change it. You'll get another one. Your classmates will help you." You know, those kinds of things. Those kinds of comments build that community, that sense of community.

Visiting Staff Developer: It's so wonderful—I am always amazed how comfortable—when I go in as a visitor to a classroom and the kids are comfortable with the visitors. And all the kids that I approached explained [to me], "Oh sure, I'll tell you," and it was wonderful that they could share their learning with the adults so easily. That is great, too.

Katherine: That's good. That's become the culture of this school . . .

In District 2 classroom visitors are a common occurrence. It is expected that students will be able to explain their work and their thinking when asked. We have found that this policy promotes true accountability among educators and students and at the same time motivates students to be active learners.

The postconference was just seventeen minutes long.

Chapter Eight

The Principal

The principal's centrality to the quality, type, and structure of staff development at a given school cannot be overstated. With the principal's support, it is possible to create mechanisms for effective onsite staff development despite the challenges faced by many of today's schools. As the lead educator in the building, the principal ultimately decides what the priorities for that school will be and articulates the goals. As the administrator, the principal sets the schedule, allocates resources, and evaluates teacher performance. The principal is key in determining what staff development will be offered at the site, with whom, for how long, and to what end. The principal's values, style, management protocols, philosophy of teaching, and beliefs about learning will affect the coach's work. It is therefore essential that the coach and the principal develop a good working rapport, establish clear channels of communication, and respect each other's roles and perspectives. Based on the work and experience in District 2, in this chapter we suggest issues for coaches and principals to take into account when thinking about the kind of communication and collaboration necessary to implement Content-Focused Coaching.

Meeting the Principal

The first meeting with the principal gives the coach the opportunity to glean insights into the school culture and establish a working relationship. It is an information-gathering session designed to set the foundation for cocreating a plan of action that will elevate the teaching and learning of mathematics over the long haul.

Bearing in mind questions like the following will help the coach gain a sense of the principal's goals, priorities, and management style:

- What is your view of the quality of mathematics teaching and learning at this school?
- What would you like to see improved?
- Have teachers expressed specific needs?
- How can I best serve the teachers at this school?
- What are your concerns about beginning a mathematics initiative in the school?
- Do you have suggestions for first steps?
- What obstacles or challenges are likely? (This question lets the principal give the coach a heads-up about potential frustrations and a chance to bypass them where possible. It also seeds the ground for collegial problem solving.)
- What are your goals in relation to mathematics instruction?
- What would be helpful for me to know about the student population? The parent population?
- How are the test scores and what is your position in relation to the importance of testing? What is the nature and extent of the school's test preparation?
- How do you prefer to work with staff developers? Do you like to meet on a regular basis? Do you enjoy coming to grade-level meetings? Planning sessions? Classes when staff development activities are in progress? How do you prefer to be kept informed of progress or concerns?
- Is mathematics a subject you enjoy?
- Is mathematics instruction something you feel comfortable evaluating?

These questions are not in any particular order. Not all of them will feel appropriate to ask at the first meeting. It is extremely important that the coach exude a genuine and nonthreatening interest in the school and the principal. The coach must not appear to be interrogating the principal or to be condescending or patronizing in any way. These behaviors are common pitfalls among coaches and they take sensitivity to avoid.

Constructing a Picture of the School

During the first and subsequent meetings with the principal, the coach constructs a picture of the school's culture and the principal's style. It is crucial to think of the school as a dynamic system in which each action affects all of the interconnected and interrelated parts. Change is not linear nor fully predictable—the whole must be kept in mind when interacting with the various parts. Consider some of the following questions to develop a sense of the big picture and the implications for staff development at a given site:

- Does the principal articulate a clear and coherent teaching/learning philosophy and suggest that the entire teaching staff is aligned with this view? If so, you will probably find that most teachers on staff have similar views and practices. In alternative schools founded on progressive ideals, for example, the principal and staff generally share a similar perspective and you are likely to enjoy a high level of cooperation.

- Does the principal profess that teaching is an eclectic practice best left to the teachers and that discordant views of teaching and learning can be found among the staff? If this is the case, cocreating a vision of excellent mathematics instruction may require more time and finesse. Gathering information about the varying values, views, styles, and goals of individual teachers could be a major focus for you in the early stages of the work.

- Does the principal practice a "hands-off" or a "hands-on" management style when it comes to instruction? A hands-on style will likely place more demands on you to keep the principal informed, but at the same time will give you more opportunities to invite the principal to participate in staff development activities. A hands-off style both allows more freedom and implies less support. The principal may be reticent to intercede if there are difficulties.

- What instructional issues does the principal intend to focus on during the school year? Is mathematics a high or low priority? If the principal views the first year as a time to seed the mathematics initiative in a few willing classrooms, for example, this may not be the year in which whole-staff meetings and grade-level meetings will be devoted to mathematics. It will be a year for establishing relationships and working to develop three or four "model" classrooms that can be used as resources next year, when mathematics, hopefully, has a more central focus.

- How does the principal view the current practice of mathematics teaching in his or her school? How does he or she evaluate student performance? If the principal is mostly satisfied with the status quo, take a close look at current practice to determine how much you agree with it. If you believe there is room for improvement one important strategy is for the coach and principal to observe classes together to discuss mathematics instruction with an eye toward finding common ground.

- Does the principal have a plan for improving mathematics teaching and learning, does she expect you to offer a plan, or does she believe that a plan will emerge through dialogue and discussion with the staff? Be prepared to offer suggestions and take the lead if asked. It makes sense to offer ideas as suggestions best to be discussed with the staff. The more teachers are invited to voice their concerns and express their needs, the more likely they are to be willing participants in the plan that's chosen.

Taking the pulse of the school in this manner will give you a window into where and how to begin the work. It is also useful to notice what is on the walls in the hallways and in the classrooms. Pay attention to room arrangements and observe student discourse both in classrooms and in the hallways. Tune in to how people speak to each other and what they talk about. By observing, asking, and listening, you will begin to develop a feel for the school's culture and norms.

Considering Each Teacher

It makes sense for the principal to sit with the coach and discuss each staff member, share insights, and consider the teacher's readiness to begin the journey of improving mathematics instruction. If the principal is willing to answer questions like the following, you can offer suggestions about the ways that individual teachers could be included in the professional development landscape:

- Does this teacher have an affinity for mathematics? Does the teacher appear to have robust content knowledge? Does she appear to enjoy teaching mathematics and teach it daily? Identify teachers who are enthusiastic about mathematics and who have some content knowledge. If you start with people with these characteristics, you will be able to develop a cadre of teacher leaders in a relatively short period of time.

- Is this teacher interested in improving her practice? Does she have a disposition for learning? Identify teachers with the disposition to become leaders who will be willing to take courses and attend conferences, workshops, and study groups.

- What is the teacher's pedagogical bent? Is she child centered or subject centered? Teachers who are intrigued by the challenge of reaching every student and who are willing to go to great lengths to find or create methods that work for even their most puzzling students are ideal candidates for coaching.

- Is this teacher a team player? How well and with which colleagues does she collaborate? The whole idea is to develop a community of learners among the teaching staff. People who like people and are social by nature tend to have good interpersonal skills and can often inspire reticent colleagues to give something new a try.

- Does the principal have a specific concern about or goal for this teacher's professional growth? Those who are invested in teaching as a profession—who want to grow and would appreciate opportunities to learn—are ideal candidates for coaching. Coaching seeks to develop the habit of reflective practice. Ideally, the teachers selected for coaching will be ready to become leaders—but they don't need to be perfect. They may need to work on their class management strategies or content knowledge or room environment. If they are self-reflective and recognize their own shortcomings, they are likely to be very good candidates for coaching.

- In what other initiatives is the teacher already involved? Often the very people you'll want to work with will already be involved in two or three other initiatives. It is important not to overburden those who have a tendency to volunteer or to overlook those who may be a bit shy or lacking in confidence.

Constructive, informative conversations about the staff give the coach opportunities to become familiar with the teachers and let the principal develop awareness of the level of knowledge she has about each teacher.

Selecting Teachers

The steps for selecting teachers to be coached are specific to the school and will be facilitated by the principal. There are three basic scenarios for getting started:

- The principal and coach walk through the building together. The principal introduces the coach to staff members who have been identified as potential candidates for initial classroom-based staff development efforts. The teachers and the coach set up appointments to explore the idea of working together.

- The principal has private conversations with the teachers she is inviting to participate in order to determine their willingness to engage in classroom-based coaching. If this is done, it is helpful for the coach and principal to establish criteria for selection and to be specific about the optimal nature and extent of involvement. Once agreement is reached, the coach is invited to meet with the selected teachers and observe in their classes.

- The coach is introduced to the entire staff at a meeting and she or the principal invites the teachers to talk with the principal if they are interested in participating in classroom-based coaching. In this scenario the coach has an opportunity to articulate an ideal scenario and begin cocreating the vision of the work with the teachers. She can present herself as an ally and colleague and assure people that she is there to serve their needs, not to impose her views upon them.

All of these scenarios are workable. The best approach depends on the school's culture and the principal's leadership style. The coach needs to be flexible and responsive to the principal's lead.

Principal Priorities Versus Coach Priorities

In choosing which teachers will receive coaching, long- and short-term goals as well as principal and staff development priorities must be balanced. In talking with the principal, the coach is looking to identify teachers with the potential to become teacher leaders. "Working from strength" should be the motto, but the principal may have different criteria than the coach does for who should be selected. For example, the principal might want to use the staff developer to support a number of new teachers, while the coach might want to work with willing veteran teachers who have the potential to become leaders within a year or two. It is possible to balance both the principal's need to support the new teachers and the coach's objective of building leadership. If the principal and the coach communicate their priorities, a compromise can be reached that will probably include a combination of teachers—some new, some veterans with high leadership potential— and a variety of structures and formats to address their different needs.

The principal and coach need to be able to negotiate a plan that considers all of their conflicting demands and priorities and keeps in mind the long-term goal. The principal's perspective adds several dimensions to the dialogue that the coach may be unaware of. Anna Switzer, the principal of PS 234, one of New York City's top-five performing schools and a former staff developer, expresses the principal's point of view:

> Sometimes a compromise has to be made. A principal may have demands a staff developer doesn't understand. I have to help this person because I promised I would. Parents are looking hard at that class. This is the first time on the grade level for a given teacher. The teacher is performing in an unsatisfactory manner and I have to show that I did something to support her.

Often the principal wants the coach to work with a teacher whose performance is problematic but who is unwilling to devote the time and energy needed for improvement. The coach needs to acknowledge that this is a valid concern because the children in that class are probably not receiving quality mathematics instruction. The coach and principal need to find a way to include such teachers in the process of change while focusing the coach's time and energy on teachers who are ready and willing to participate.

One option that has worked in District 2 is for the principal to arrange for the teacher in question to observe the coach working in another classroom and to attend follow-up debriefing conferences. This approach often gives a teacher a chance to consider change without being pressured to perform. Trusting the process and working with teachers in ways they are willing to engage in are crucial tenets in effective coaching. Anna Switzer concurs with the idea that coaches need to engage most of their energies with strong, willing teachers while we work to bring everyone along:

> In my opinion, you don't help the weakest teacher until everyone else is on board—until you train people to be fabulous leaders and the average teacher to do their job well. The weakest people should always be invited and they should be expected to come, but that is not where to focus for long-term results.

The long-term goal of coaching is to create a collaborative professional community. Even though the coach is in the business of nurturing potential leaders and it is unlikely that people who resist change will emerge as leaders in the first or second years of an initiative, it is important that every teacher be treated with respect and compassion. There have been cases where teachers who were skeptical and reluctant in the first couple of years became excellent leaders over the long haul. In these cases, the initial reluctance came either from the teacher's feeling inadequate because of tenuous content knowledge and fear of its discovery or from the teacher's being cynical because of past disappointments in getting involved with new programs.

It is important that the principal be willing to appropriately challenge senior staff members to continually develop and refine their practice. In most schools, the principal has "inherited" staff members whose views may not be harmonious with the mathematics initiative. Such teachers often have tenure, and many were viewed as "good teachers" by previous principals. It is difficult to fall from grace with aplomb. Coming to terms with the idea that one's previously satisfactory performance now needs improvement is challenging for most people. Anna Marie Carrillo, the principal of PS 116, a successful inner-city school serving a diverse and challenging population, was quite resourceful in working with such teachers. She would observe a teacher giving a lesson, then accompany that teacher to the room of a colleague who was teaching the same lesson to a similar group of students, suggesting that the first teacher listen to the student discourse. Here she describes one teacher's reaction to this experience:

> One of my teachers who will never be the most reflective came to me after this kind of experience and said, "I am embarrassed by the students I graduated in June. Now that I know what they could have known, it is shameful. The kids had no clue what they were doing. I wasn't really teaching. How much smarter I feel I am, and what I am doing with children is so much more important.

Building Consensus

The design and orchestration of staff development work depends on how the goals for the work are conceived. It is important for the coach to work with the principal to articulate an explicit picture of what striving for excellence in mathematics education at the school will entail. When schoolwide goals are negotiated among the principal, the teachers, and the coach, they are more likely to be achieved.

The school environment needs to encourage people to express their beliefs about mathematics instruction and student learning. The principal sets the expectation that teachers will engage in conversations about teaching and learning mathematics, and encourages them to do so from a stance of curiosity and open-mindedness. An environment of high challenge and low risk is nonthreatening and productive. If long-term, schoolwide, fundamental improvement is to take root, coaches must facilitate ongoing conversations that stimulate the creative and rigorous thinking of all who are involved—including the coach. It is through intense, informed, and thoughtful conversations that the staff at a given school will evolve into a professional community. These conversations should be aimed at building a shared understanding of mathematics, of mathematics instruction, and of how children learn mathematics. By engaging teachers in mathematics, the coach can determine the depth and flexibility of each teacher's content knowledge. At the same time, teachers will deepen their understanding and further develop their pedagogical repertoire. Skillful staff development engages staff members in nonthreatening ways that help them realize where their practices don't meet students' needs. It engenders in teachers a willingness to learn more content and practice more effective methods. The principal, coach, and teachers must clarify their expectations for student performance in mathematics and determine how performance is evaluated and measured so that the entire staff will use assessment criteria that are explicit and coherent.

Relationships Among Coach, Teacher, and Principal

Staff developers often feel a tension between reporting to the principal and establishing trusting relationships with teachers. In part this worry is a product of the hierarchical, adversarial tendencies that our present education system engenders. Content-Focused Coaching offers an opportunity to change the way things are to a more productive model. What if we decide that all three players—the teacher, the coach, and the principal—would benefit from collaboratively setting goals and benchmarks that everyone is comfortable with? What if we deliberately blur the lines of authority and make central the premise that we all want to become more effective educators of the children we serve?

This view implies that the teachers who will be working with a coach have a voice in negotiating what structures will be used and what constitutes participation. More permeable role boundaries can allow us to reveal what we don't know in order to help each other become more effective educators. The coach and principal must take a stance that is as inquisitive and open-minded as the one they want teachers to take. Anna Marie Carrillo exemplifies this attitude:

> Sometimes I go with the staff developer and listen to the conversations they have in the debriefing sessions. Then when I go into classrooms I am smarter about it, because a lot of it is pushing the envelope on work that is happening for the first time in this building. If I am part of the conversation, I have a better understanding of what the goal is and how I can support it.

Anna Marie recalls a time when she included a staff developer in an observation of a lesson:

> I remember asking the coach to sit with me as I was observing a second-grade class. I didn't have a handle on what was really going on here. The coach walked me through the lesson. I found it was extremely helpful.

It takes courage and humility to admit that you require assistance, especially if you're supposed to be the leader. In this instance, Anna Marie decided to utilize the staff developer for her own learning and thereby set the example that learning is a great way to lead.

Consider that most principals are not confident mathematicians and may not be clear about how to best evaluate a mathematics lesson. One way to build a common view of what constitutes effective mathematics instruction and to develop trusting relationships is for the principal to participate in the planning dialogues and observe the lessons the coach and teachers are working on. These observations are done outside of the official evaluative observation most principals are required to do. After the lesson, all parties discuss their perceptions and raise questions as they endeavor to understand and refine mathematics teaching and learning. Anna Switzer has found that accompanying the staff developer as she works with teachers is beneficial to her work as principal:

> What I learned last year from going with the staff developers into math classes is that there were things I didn't understand. When I didn't understand certain content, I didn't always make the right conclusion about what I saw.

This practice demonstrates to staff that the principal is aware of the halting, tentative, sometimes frustrating nature of significant change and is willing to be a participant in the process rather than a demanding authority.

Tracking Progress

On the other hand, the principal's inviting the staff developer to observe a class with her raises an important and sensitive issue that needs to be discussed: What is the coach's role in teacher evaluation? All parties involved need explicit, specific feedback about their progress. This raises an essential question: How will progress be measured? Progress is messy and often sporadic. Transitioning from one style of teaching to another or attempting to master new content or implement a new curriculum can catapult a teacher onto a steep learning trajectory. Mistakes are part of the process, and at the beginning skills are at a low level. It is important that principals don't mistake fledgling attempts at change for poor teaching. During a change process, what the principal will evaluate must be determined through a great deal of conversation and reflection. The principal must not inadvertently disrupt work that is just beginning to take root.

Though the role of the coach is primarily to assist teachers and not to evaluate them, clear ongoing feedback about progress is essential. The principal must be kept apprised of the work because she is responsible for the school's quality of teaching, which affects the extent of student learning. Anna Switzer has been a pioneer in establishing effective relationships among the principal, the staff developer, and teachers. She describes her thinking:

> This is professional work—it is not personal. I tell teachers, "See the staff developer as your lifeline. Staff developers are expensive, incredible resources: Use them well." The principal does not want to know every false step, she wants to know progress over time. The principal has to follow through, the staff developer needs to deliver, and the teacher needs to learn.

Anna Marie Carrillo talks about the emotions that are involved in these relationships:

> This issue of people not being afraid of the staff developer and administrator is such an important thing. It allows people to become willing to take risks; saying what they need, being open to what support is available for them. It is such an important thing, and for staff developers to feel like they can trust you [the principal] and to say what they need to have happen is so important.

In essence there is a three-way contract between teacher, principal, and staff developer. The more explicit and specific the agreement is, the less likely there will be miscommunications. Progress is more likely when people are clear about what is expected.

When Problems Arise

The principal and the coach need to communicate regularly and often about the work and establish protocols for doing so. When something is amiss, it should not be allowed to fester. The principal should be informed early on when the coach has tried to work out problems with a teacher one-on-one. Sometimes the principal will have helpful suggestions or will schedule a three-way meeting to resolve problems. The coach is at a bit of a disadvantage when things do not go well because she is often seen as an outsider. Anna Switzer suggests:

> Noncommunication is a big issue, because I don't think staff developers are brought into the school as members of the school community enough. They should come to the first staff meeting. And the principal should attend their grade-level meetings. And they should receive all the mail and be invited on retreats. And frequent conversations and communication should occur. A note in the principal's mailbox once a week is helpful.

Establishing communication ground rules and practicing them is not always easy, but it can prevent major misunderstandings. Cultivating interpersonal and communication skills is essential for any successful coach.

Scheduling and Logistics

Time

Although focused and constructive professional discourse may be one of the most important ingredients in improving teaching and learning, most public school schedules don't allow for such discourse, which requires regular, structured time. Teachers may or may not have a preparation period each day. They may or may not view preparation periods, lunch periods, or time after school as time to meet and plan with a coach or colleagues. Contract restrictions may dictate teachers' use of time.

Time is one of the biggest constraints in this process. In the long run, it is likely that the professional day will need to be reorganized, and perhaps lengthened, if collaborative planning and reflective practice are to become the norm. In the short term, creative scheduling is a practical strategy for making time for professional learning. Some principals are quite creative in carving out time for planning and reflection. One way is to schedule lunch periods and preparation periods back-to-back one day a week for each grade level. The teachers bring their lunches and their student work or a lesson plan to a weekly grade-level meeting. The principal provides dessert and beverages. Sometimes money can be budgeted to pay teachers to meet after school one day a week. In some cases, teachers find the work so valuable that they choose to meet before or after school without pay.

As soon as possible, the coach and the principal should consider scheduling and logistics and work on formats that will allow for teacher intervisitations, planning and reflecting times, grade-level meetings, and all-staff events. The schedules that are the most conducive to the work are created with professional development as a top priority and with principal, staff developer, and teachers collaboratively constructing solutions to time constraints. This rarely happens. Often the schedule has been made prior to planning the staff development, so staff development activities must be woven into a schedule in which lunch duty, union restrictions, and the like are priorities. This can cause many glitches in the successful implementation of a reliable and effective professional development schedule.

One benchmark of real change is when the principal insists that teaching and learning be given top priority, especially in the creation of the school schedule. The psychology is subtle, but the effects are profound: When your purpose is clear, your actions are in sync. For example, it is imperative that each teacher who is working with a coach be given time to talk about the work with the coach. When the principal recognizes the relevance of such "talk time" she will schedule for it even if several challenges have to be overcome to do so.

Professionals need to examine how the use of time affects teaching and learning and keep in mind that the business of education is the business of learning. Asking "Does this activity or schedule contribute to student learning?" is one way to prioritize the use of time.

Money

Budgeting may not seem relevant to staff developers, but becoming cognizant of budgeting and time constraints helps the coach develop a "big picture" view of the school's priorities that lets her be part of the solution instead of one more demanding voice in the principal's ear. Often in District 2, the mathematics staff developer and either the principal or her designee collaboratively create the budget for staff development at the beginning of the school year.

It is wise to arrange for at least one other teacher of the same grade level to observe in the classroom in which the coach is working and to sit in on at least some of the planning and debriefing sessions. This is cost effective, though it often requires hiring a substitute teacher to provide coverage on coaching days. We've known staff developers who have helped principals obtain small grants to cover the cost of substitutes or to provide after-school workshops and intervisitations for teachers.

Pesky Details

The success of the coach's efforts will depend in large part on establishing a working relationship with the principal that acknowledges the nuts and bolts of school life. Principals are responsible for all aspects of teaching and learning as well as safety, budget, scheduling, community relations, and the demands of the district office. The coach must remember that mathematics may not always be the principal's highest priority. For example, early in an initiative the coach may realize that supplies are needed. The coach should learn how to request the necessary materials and who is responsible for ordering and distributing them when they arrive, a process that varies from school to school. The coach needs to be mindful of the long-term goal and remove obstacles. If she is aware that needed materials are lacking, she might offer to make a list of required supplies or type up the purchase order and distribute the goods when they arrive. This kind of work should not constitute the bulk of a coach's time and energy, but attention to these kinds of details can build collegial relations and ensure the success of the work.

Asking early on about procedures for purchasing materials, duplicating articles or work assignments, reserving meeting space, purchasing snacks or beverages for meetings, and myriad other details requires friendly communications and a problem-solving attitude. Anna Switzer suggests that a coach's "nonrespect" for the principal's role is at the root of many miscommunications:

Nonrespect for the role of the principal might play out in a number of ways. One is that the staff developer might not understand why the principal couldn't meet with her every week. The staff developer might go to the principal saying that something the principal promised to order has not been ordered, instead of asking how she could help secure the order, even if it means typing up the purchase order. Sometimes there simply was not a specific plan in place to get the job done. Sometimes staff developers have to be generalists, give out the books, and Xerox the handout, write the parent newsletters.

Anna is not suggesting that staff developers be assigned clerical responsibilities, but they need to be pragmatic problem solvers who are clear in their purpose and willing to do what needs doing to get the job done. "Remove all obstacles" is one of our guiding mantras.

Information is power, and lack of information leads to miscommunication and avoidable difficulties. It is important to discuss how much and how often the principal expects to be kept apprised of the staff developer's work and progress. Some principals want the staff developer to pop into the office for a quick hello whenever she is in the building. Some want formal weekly meetings, while others prefer a note in their mailbox at the end of the day. It is wise for the coach to ask questions like the following early on in the intiative:

- How does the principal prefer to be kept apprised of the coach's work? (A note in her mailbox, an informal visit at the end of the day, etc.)
- How will staff members communicate with the coach? (Through a mailbox in the office, email message, phone calls, etc.)
- Who should the coach notify if she will be absent or late?
- Who at the school will notify teachers if the coach will be absent or late?
- What is the protocol for notifying the coach that her schedule will be interrupted by class trips or other school events?
- Who is responsible for adjusting the coach's schedule if one of the teachers she normally works with is out?
- What is the protocol for duplicating necessary materials?
- Is there a desk, closet, computer, and telephone that the coach can use?

Inevitably, there will be unforeseen problems with the schedule. What if a teacher is absent on a day the staff developer is scheduled to meet with her? What if the substitute doesn't show up? What if the schedule looks good on paper but just doesn't work? These are the kinds of details that require collaboration and cheerful perseverance.

It often takes a couple of months before a coaching intiative can settle into a predictable routine.

The point is that staff development is not about ego and it's not about territory. It is about doing whatever it takes to improve teaching and learning. It's a bigger waste of time to not have materials ready when they're needed than to spend five minutes running off thirty copies of a worksheet to ensure a successful lesson. The by-product of this kind of humility and cooperation is respectful, fruitful relationships. And a successful staff development initiative is all about relationships.

Chapter Nine

The District

Planning, implementing, and funding professional development is a school district responsibility. Onsite professional development is an expensive endeavor that requires a long-term financial commitment. It is highly likely that if a district is embarking on a course that includes Content-Focused Coaching, the district's leadership team understands the importance of investing in professional development—and that onsite coaching is only one of the professional development opportunities available to teachers. The superintendent of such a district, probably believes that a collaborative and reflective culture will ultimately result in improved teaching and learning that manifests as high student achievement.

It is the superintendent's job to establish a district's course of change. This requires that all the educators involved in the process create a shared vision of effective teaching and agree on criteria for evidence of learning. Content-Focused Coaching provides a framework for the type of dialogue that can engage educators at every level to cocreate this shared vision and an understanding of the knowledge base to work toward this vision. Ultimately, by focusing conversation on the core issues of lesson planning, implementation, and learning assessment, the coach acts as a catalyst for improvement throughout the district.

In this chapter we share lessons learned in our efforts to integrate Content-Focused Coaching into New York City's Community School District 2. The implementation of Content-Focused Coaching in the district has been based on a clear vision for developing multilayered learning communities in which professional learning is valued alongside student learning. We advocate not that people attempt to directly imitate what is happening in District 2, but rather that they consider the conditions that are necessary to provide effective professional development that results in improved student achievement and an ongoing professional learning community.

Content-Focused Coaching will be most powerful if it is woven into a whole network of staff development activities that are coherently related. For example, teachers and coaches should also work together in staff development workshops and study groups that deepen both content knowledge and pedagogical content knowledge. Coaching and workshop sessions can thus mutually support each other.

For a practice like Content-Focused Coaching to successfully develop within a school district and for the district to take advantage of its catalytic function for building a professional culture, the element of coaching has to be understood in its relationship to other elements of professional development at the school and district levels. Classroom-based coaching needs to be carefully incorporated into the staff development work within both school and district. Preconditions include establishing trusting relationships. Depending on a district's history, the extent of common experience and the amount of shared knowledge among personnel may vary to a great extent. These variations result in different levels of trust between teachers and coaches. Such differences need to be taken into account when implementing Content-Focused Coaching.

Another prerequisite is developing organizational structures that allow teachers to first enter the process of Content-Focused Coaching as peripheral participants, such as observers. In District 2, coaching sessions are organized in such a way that the coaching of one teacher can also be used as an opportunity for other teachers to learn from each other. Teacher colleagues can observe lessons and participate in postlesson reflections on days when the coach is present. Less formally, they can do the same thing without the coach when teachers identify something they want to explore together.

Situating the Coach in the District Hierarchy

Full-time coaches in District 2 occupy a unique position in the school bureaucracy. Though they tend to report to someone at the central office, they work in schools with principals and teachers. They are not supervisors and do not have line authority over teachers, and principals generally do not have authority over coaches. The fact that the coach occupies an ambiguous place in the district's power structure offers potential rather than limitation. In District 2 we found that the most influential change agents are people who are willing to "think outside the box" and reach past customary role boundaries to cocreate structures and strategies that serve student learning.

In District 2, content-focused coaches also plan and implement staff development activities in more traditional settings, such as districtwide workshops. The links among coaches' different tasks is very powerful because the design and implementation of districtwide staff development is informed and based on the coaches' extensive experience in coaching teachers. Coaches serve as conduits between the schools and the district office because they provide a feedback loop to the leadership team about how district policy is playing out in the field. We do not mean that staff developers serve as district spies, but rather that they provide district leaders with information about what professional development and materials are needed based on their close interactions with teachers and children throughout the district. Because they work in many schools, staff developers are often the first to discern a need for learning or a district trend or issue. Their feedback can help the district make sensible adjustments or provide support. In District 2, for example, it became evident that teachers were feeling frustrated because they seemed to be receiving double messages. The literacy staff developers were helping them design classrooms in which all of the blackboards were covered and used to display children's work and other relevant materials. The mathematics staff developers were encouraging them to uncover six to eight feet of blackboard space so that they would be able to lay out a footprint of the mathematics lesson as students shared their problem-solving strategies. When this contradiction was brought to the fore, the district leadership team saw the wisdom of bringing the math and literacy staff developers together periodically to discuss this and other issues related to the work. These meetings resulted in more clarity at the district level about what was needed to successfully interweave the mathematics and literacy professional development initiatives. The coach is a member of several layers of the learning community—she often is included in the principal's conferences, meets with teachers, meets with other coaches, and meets with district-level staff—and thus is in a uniquely powerful position to contribute to the development of professional learning communities. She is also both a teacher and a learner, depending on the setting in which she finds herself. Coaches play a privotal role in creating what has been termed "nested learning communities" (Fink & Resnick 2001; Resnick & Hall 1998).

This is a unique time for coaches and staff developers in many districts because their roles are now being defined. At the same time, knowledgeable coaches appear to be in demand. As districts place more emphasis on professional development, the roles of staff developers will evolve. Those of us who are in the field should be proactive advocates for creating the settings and role responsibilities that are most likely to result in improvement of teaching and learning.

Developing a Professional Community

Lee Shulman (1998, 516) notes that an essential characteristic of any profession is "a professional community to monitor quality and aggregate knowledge." However, most teachers work alone and behind closed doors. Where is the professional community in this scenario? Coaches have a key role to play in developing professional communities. They play a pivotal role in nurturing environments where rigorous analysis, healthy risk-taking, and reflective practice can flourish. A coach gets observed teaching a lesson, and through coaching dialogues presents his thinking about the lesson plan and the choices made during the lesson for scrutiny by others. In this way, the coach models the kinds of conversations that stimulate the thinking of all involved, thus providing an example of what it means to engage in a professional community.

The coach models professional commitment by initiating dialogues that focus on the teaching and learning of mathematics, implementing lessons or coteaching lessons with teachers, and then reflecting on the lessons. She brings the most up-to-date research around best practice to bear on these conversations. She frames the conversations around principles of learning and evidence of student achievement. Any one school is too insular and homogeneous to ensure significant systemic progress because its staff members' experiences are common and their views are likely to be unchallenged. Engaging in professional conversations in which diverse and often divergent views are expressed, considered, and evaluated induces growth. Yet it is rare for teachers to visit each other in their own schools and rarer still for them to visit teachers in neighboring schools. The coach has a key role to play in extending the professional community beyond the borders of a single school. Coaches must hold up opposing views for scrutiny and engender dialogue that encourages others to do the same. Coaches must keep abreast of the professional development offerings within and outside of the district and bring that information to school and district personnel. Effective coaches also link the schools they work with by creating opportunities for teachers from one school to visit colleagues at another. They provide forums for teachers to talk with others from across the district about mathematics content, instruction, and assessment.

This professional community is further developed when leaders visit schools and classrooms on a regular basis. The coach has a significant role to play by bringing principals and relevant district personnel together to observe mathematics lessons. Coaches need to encourage these personnel to take a stance of curiosity as they look at and listen to classroom discourse; study student work; talk with students about what they are learning; and question, question, question each other and teachers and students about interactions, practices, strategies, content, assessments, and pedagogy. Through this process, coaches help to develop a shared clarity about what constitutes good mathematics instruction and involve everyone in cocreating learning environments in which students thrive. These ongoing conversations will lead the entire learning community to gradually become smarter about teaching and learning.

The tone of these conversations should be one of mutual respect and inquiry. They are not meant to be evaluative in the sense of rating teachers on performance. Instead, they are designed to ensure that principals, district personnel, staff developers, and teachers have similar values and criteria for excellence. The more coherent the vision, the more likely that it will be implemented and articulated to the larger community.

Once this long-term vision has been established, district leaders need to take stock of what is happening in mathematics instruction and begin setting short-term goals. The coach's work is important to these short-term plans. It is the coach who engages teachers in the change process and guides that process at the classroom level. The coach is in a prime position to take stock of what is going on in classrooms. In theory, the coach also has flexible, deep content knowledge and can ascertain the level of mathematics content in the lessons observed. Thus the coach is uniquely qualified to identify the scope and nature of the professional development activities that would be most beneficial.

Coaches are also in an excellent position to identify the teachers who are most likely to emerge as leaders and to serve as their mentors. Prospective coaches can be nurtured from within the ranks of a district's teachers over a period of two or three years if they are identified early and are among the first to receive the support of Content-Focused Coaching. In this "building from strength" model of change you work with the strongest, most enthusiastic teachers first because they will become the leaders in their schools. The process is an ongoing, long-term journey that requires strategic planning.

Deciding where to place coaches is a complex decision. Should the effort be launched in a few schools to begin with? Should coaches work at a particular grade level in all schools? Should coaches work with volunteers at any grade level at any school? Bea Johnstone, deputy superintendent of District 2, describes the strategy used during the early stages of the district's mathematics initiative:

> I think what we did was combine two schools that were a little further along with two schools that needed more support. The thinking behind that was developing a mentoring relationship in which people could see work that was being done in classrooms that were

maybe two steps more advanced than what was being done in their classrooms. Katherine [the staff developer] would bring teachers from these two schools together and work with them individually—modeling lessons, bringing them for intervisitations, debriefing—sort of like the model we have now—only it's much more expansive at this point.

The district focused its resources on select schools with the intention of getting several classrooms functioning in ways that could serve as models for teachers from around the district to visit.

Regardless of the model to be followed, there are a number of questions that will influence how to implement Content-Focused Coaching at a given school.

- Who is initiating the idea for mathematics reform?

- Is the principal seeking mathematics support at the request of a number of teachers? If there are a number of teachers asking for help, there will be obvious candidates to begin working with.

- Does the principal perceive the need for improvement or is the pressure to get help coming from the district office? If the principal wants the program, he is likely to find the time and create the structures needed to make it work. If the district is pressuring the principal who has reservations to implement Content-Focused Coaching, the coach will have to focus more attention on working with the principal to find common ground.

- Is this the first time that onsite staff development will be used at this school? If so, it needs to be made clear up front that professional dialogues around teaching and learning are valued and are not geared at teachers who are considered problematic.

- What are the demographics of the students? For example, if there is a large second-language population, the coach needs to be aware of resources for translating materials for students and parents.

- What is the experience range of the teachers? If the school is staffed predominantly by new teachers, the coach may want to consider group conferences or after-school minicourses to support teachers.

- In what other academic staff development initiatives is the school engaged? Which teachers are heavily involved in them?

- How are any competing initiatives structured and scheduled? Coordinating initiatives takes conscious effort and a long-term view.

- Does the staff talk about teaching and learning on a regular basis in both formal and informal settings, such as in the hallways and at grade-level meetings? If they do, this school should be easy to work in. If not, building a culture in which talking about teaching and learning is the norm may take time.

- What are the academic priorities and what rank is given to mathematics?
- Is there a curriculum that all teachers follow? Are the teachers expected to follow a pacing schedule? Are these things negotiable? If everyone uses the same materials, it is easier to share experiences; if not, discussions about selection of materials and tasks may be needed to reach consensus on specific lessons.

In other words, how conducive is the school's culture to mathematics professional development? The district also needs to be alert for red flags that may present challenges for onsite staff development:

- A principal who has a piecemeal approach to staff development or a "flavor of the month" perspective.
- A principal who sees staff development as a way to "fix" bad teachers and who will abdicate her responsibility to challenge and support teachers in appropriate ways.
- A staff that is already focused on other major initiatives will most likely feel stretched and find it difficult to devote the necessary time to mathematics improvement.
- A staff that isn't open to professional development in mathematics because the students' scores on standardized tests are high.
- Parent bodies that aren't ready for changes in mathematics instruction because standardized test scores are high.
- Staff members who view teaching as an independent endeavor and maintain teacher-centered classrooms in which they do their own thing and see no reason to change.
- A competitive school culture in which some teachers are seen as "stars" and teaching is viewed as an idiosyncratic art that belongs to those "born to teach."
- Staff members who are bound by nonnegotiable union rules and who don't have ongoing good communication with the principal guided by the shared goal of working on improving student learning.

Considering each of the schools in a district in light of these questions will enable the district team to see the big picture and prepare for the different dynamics and strategies needed for long-term success. While someone on the district team will decide which schools get mathematics professional development and which coaches are assigned to those schools, coaches are not powerless in this process. They should be proactive and inform their supervisors of their preferences, passions, and strengths. For example, some coaches prefer to work with schools that are struggling to turn around a negative trend, while others are interested in refining teaching strategies and lessons in schools where there is already a strong collaborative culture. One coach may be more successful with a principal who has a hands-off policy, while another cherishes the direct style of a different principal. By making their preferences known, coaches do their part to help the district make the best possible match between school and coach.

A perfect match is never guaranteed, however, so it is incumbent upon coaches to understand who at the district they can turn to if the situation at their school becomes problematic. This is a delicate issue and protocols are often not spelled out until after the fact. The coach is in a precarious position because often there is no one to advocate on the coach's behalf. It is important to establish a communication system early and to maintain it regularly. For example, the coach might write a note to the principal each week about the work that was done and send a copy to his supervisor at the district office. The coach should schedule regular meetings with his supervisor to discuss the work at the various schools to which he is assigned. It would be in everyone's best interest for the coach, his supervisor, and the principal to meet on occasion and perhaps to visit a class together. Sometimes the coach's supervisor is also the principal's supervisor. If this is the case, three-way meetings at the beginning, middle, and end of the year to set goals and discuss progress and concerns go a long way toward preventing unpleasant surprises at the end of the year. On occasion in District 2, a staff developer has been notified of a principal's dissatisfaction at the end of the school year. This information came as a surprise to both the coach and his supervisor, indicating poor communication during the year and a lack of protocol for handling differences.

In Closing

The caveat in any of these strategies for beginning systemic change is that the gap between those who are participating and those who are not will widen. Volunteerism reinforces the notion that individual teachers have the right to do their own thing without responsibility to the professional community or regard for the interdependence of the system. It also reinforces the notion that teaching is an idiosyncratic art that is not replicable on a large scale. Learning is a social activity; somehow we must create professional communities in which rigorous dialogues on teaching and learning are the norm. If improvement is going to take root, then everyone will eventually have to participate

(Elmore 2001). The question becomes, how do we invite participation in a way that is respectful of both the individual and the community? At some point along the way the district is likely to find itself saying, "It is simply unacceptable to opt out." Volunteerism is a beginning strategy, but it cannot remain an option. In order to ensure that all students get high levels of instruction, all teachers must continue to hone their practice. In order for all students to achieve at high levels, all teachers must have the repertoire of skills and knowledge needed to teach at high levels.

Transformation takes time and patience, courage and perseverance. There should be multiple entry points for teachers, and a variety of structures that give teachers at different levels and different points in their careers the chance to get involved. Little on the road to change is static and the journey of continuous improvement requires readjusting our sails time and time again (Fullan 1999). As we learn more together we are able to improve our collective practice.

Chapter Ten

From Teacher to Coach

This chapter briefly describes the process used in District 2 to select and develop coaches in order to give you a sense of the kind of support that helps teachers transition to coaching positions. Testimony from coaches now working in District 2 provides a taste of some of the typical challenges and feelings that teachers experience when they move from classroom positions to coaching positions. We also share voices from the field to describe strategies that coaches have experimented with using to address challenges, the ways that coaches determine the impact they are having on others, and the growth they can identify in themselves.

Making the Transition

Ideally, content-focused coaches are experienced staff developers or teachers with expertise in specific content areas, and they have knowledge in adult learning. In District 2, math coaches need to have a minimum of five years of teaching experience, one year as a teacher leader and at least three years of active, intense participation in professional development offerings in mathematics. Content expertise and the coach's motivation to deepen his or her content knowledge as it relates to teaching are pivotal for the kind of practice we envision. The demand for highly qualified coaches is now greater than the supply, so it is likely that a cadre of coaches will need to be nurtured from within the district over a period of years. In District 2, the ratio of coaches hired from outside the district to coaches hired from within was reversed over three years. In the early years, we had twice as many consultants as we did teachers-turned-coaches. In 2000, only four of fourteen coaches were outside consultants. We think that it will always be important to have a couple of outside consultants as part of a team because they will provide fresh insights and prevent the team or district from becoming too insular.

The process for becoming a coach in District 2 involves being coached as a teacher for at least one full year. The experience of being coached gives a person practice in professional conversations and helps that person internalize the core issues of lesson design and become sensitive to the issues of coaching from the teacher's perspective. The coaches who were first coachees are some of the most vocal advocates for teachers. Aspiring coaches take requisite courses in both mathematics and mathematics education offered through the district in affiliation with local universities. They then become teacher leaders for a minimum of one year. Teacher leaders continue to teach children, coach one or more colleagues at their school, generally on their grade level, and facilitate grade-level or department meetings focused on mathematics on a regular basis. The teacher leader is assisted in these new responsibilities by a coach who might help plan meetings, observe coaching sessions, and provide feedback. The coaching emphasis shifts from assisting the teacher leader with students to assisting the teacher leader with colleagues. Coaches come from the ranks of teacher leaders and are invited to become coaches by the district's director of mathematics. Not all teacher leaders become coaches. In fact, most do not, because it is important not to drain the schools of knowledgeable teachers in the classroom and to have onsite expertise at the school level.

Teacher leaders and coaches attend districtwide biweekly or monthly meetings that focus on acquiring knowledge in the content area, pedagogical knowledge, pedagogical content knowledge, familiarity with curriculum, standards and assessments, learning theory, change theory, and communication and interpersonal skills. These meetings are very practical. They provide a place for coaches and teacher leaders to become skilled in using the tools and tenets of Content-Focused Coaching, among other things.

When a teacher leader is invited to become a full-time coach, she is assigned an experienced coach, who acts as her mentor. The mentor accompanies the new coach during the first month of school when she meets with the principal and teachers at the school she is assigned to. The novice coach is allotted one or two days to "shadow" her mentor in the mentor's assigned schools. This scaffolding supports the novice as she transitions from classroom teacher to staff developer.

Learning in a Coaching Team

There are weekly staff developer meetings in District 2 in which coaches of all experience levels discuss the issues they are facing in their schools. The meetings provide a place for the team to have professional conversations about the coach's role and practice. The meetings ensure coherence among and continued development of the team members.

Suzanne, a novice coach and former teacher leader, expressed an opinion about our meetings that is typical among the mathematics coaches:

> The Friday meetings were invaluable to me last year. One of the best parts for me was hearing colleagues talking about encountering problems that were plaguing me. It made me feel that even seasoned staff developers were running into the same frustrations I was. I also loved the depth of the discussion. Although I did not often speak, I found myself thinking about the issues under discussion all week. This helped to counter the superficial level of discussions in my schools.

Suzanne's comment provides a flavor of the nature of the dialogue that staff developers engage in for part of the meeting time. Problems do not turn into griping sessions, nor are they discounted or ignored. Rather, they become grist for creatively pursuing improvement. Team members glean strength and a willingness to persevere from their professional community.

Sarah provides a specific example of how one of these dialogues affected her work:

> There were several Friday mornings where staff developers were talking about being frustrated with the teachers and not being effective. Lucy talked about taking good notes, and the importance of giving people very specific feedback. The importance of giving people feedback on management and on mathematics at the same time struck me. If in fact a teacher needed help with management, that couldn't be ignored, but that couldn't be the only thing you focused on. I can certainly become better at observing both teachers and students and taking much better notes.

Sarah's tone exemplifies the learning stance that we believe is crucial for coaches. She is learning from presentations and the experience reported by colleagues, and reflecting on how she can improve her practice.

Regular, frequent meetings designed to support coaches in the practical day-to-day work of professional development are the most important vehicle for ensuring a successful mathematics initiative. In

District 2 they have kept us on course while at the same time giving us the space and time to grow and deepen our knowledge base and our network. They have given us a sense of identity and purpose and kept us going through very rocky and challenging times. The following sections describe some of the specific ways the meeting times have been used.

Collaboratively Planning Based on the Core Issues in Mathematics Lesson Planning

In the early years, when there were about six to eight staff developers working as coaches in District 2, we jointly planned workshops using the Guide to Core Issues in Mathematics Lesson Design as our map. This allowed us to consider the needs of our teachers, to become familiar with the core issues of lesson design, and to develop effective ways to incorporate the Guide to Core Issues in Mathematics Lesson Design and the Framework for Lesson Design and Analysis into our practice. These efforts resulted in very coherent workshops that were interactive, teacher empowering events. Teachers literally became our cocreators in the process of improvement. Our workshops generally involve teachers in doing the mathematics activities in the curriculum materials they teach, taking the time to analyze the mathematics together, identifying the pivotal lessons in the unit, and constructing pedagogical content knowledge that aids instruction. We spend little time telling teachers what to do, and quite a bit of time inviting teachers to collaboratively tap their own expertise. We do provide suggestions and support materials in an environment of high challenge and low risk as a way to jump-start the process of coconstruction.

Reflecting on the Coaching Work

Another practice that has had a positive impact is time spent reflecting on our practice as coaches and analyzing the schools in which we work. Coaches write midyear and end-of-year progress reflections that help determine our next steps and clarify what issues to raise with the principals of the schools we are assigned to. Sometimes we focus on one teacher to help us develop our skill at analyzing what we can do to improve our work relationships with teachers who are challenging to work with. Sarah found one of the tasks we worked on particularly helpful:

> We did a writing exercise in which we selected a teacher that we were having trouble working with. We wrote everything that we could

think of about that teacher and wrote something about our own difficulties. Then we wrote a response to ourselves from the point of
view of that teacher, and I found that extremely helpful.

Video Recording As a Tool for Reflection

Working with videotapes was consistently valuable for learning. We
videotaped ourselves coaching others and we videotaped the lessons.
During our meetings we watched segments of the coaching sessions
and lessons and analyzed which coaching moves had a positive impact on the teacher's practice. We reflected on the core issues addressed
and on our coaching styles. This helped us become more focused as
we observed lessons and to take more specific notes to use in postconference dialogues.

Extending and Refining the Knowledge Base of Teaching

Two books that we find particularly useful for collaborative study are
Making Sense: Teaching and Learning Mathematics with Understanding
(Hiebert et al. 1997) and *Knowing and Teaching Elementary Mathematics*
(Ma 1999). The first helped us refine our thinking about pedagogy and
the second helped us delve deeply into specific mathematics content.
We also spent time examining standards, curriculum materials, assess-
ments, and standardized test questions and the like to help ourselves
make connections and to ensure alignment.

Our coaches also took such courses as Lenses on Learning (Grant,
et al. 2002a) and Developing Mathematical Ideas (Schifter et al. 1999a
and b) in teams of two or four. Participants later taught the courses
to our colleagues as a way of deepening and broadening our pedagogical content knowledge. All coaches participated in lesson study activities and found ways to interweave the format of lesson study and the
tenets of Content-Focused Coaching. We continued to look outward
and avail ourselves of the latest developments in the field while challenging ourselves to incorporate what we learned from others into the
work in District 2.

Common Challenges

We offer here some voices from the field expressing their frustrations
and challenges. The coaches that we work with have often commented

on how comforting it is to know that they are not alone in feeling inadequate or uncertain. In the spirit of providing some comfort to our readers, we include here the authentic voices of practicing coaches talking about specific issues they struggle with.

> Day to day I rethink my position and wonder if I like it or not, or if I think I am good enough, and it always changes. One of the biggest surprises was now I was not just a teacher anymore—or so people think. And the truth is, I am more of a learner now than before and I like that part of the job. But people really trust you and believe that you will have answers or advice for them about anything they need. And surprisingly, it is like feeding the whole village with two loaves of bread and a few fish: You just keep finding ideas and things that you didn't know you had when you focus and apply yourself.
>
> —Karen

> I think the piece that's hardest for me is being so scattered with so many different teachers, and so many different subjects, and so many different grade levels that I don't have follow-through. The goal was for me to work with as many people who were willing to work with me because in the past there was resistance. But I got more people who were willing to work with me than I expected and, thinking about it, more than I could realistically handle.
>
> —Charlene

> Having just come out of the classroom, I was very sensitive to the amount of staff development our teachers are expected to take part in (the word *endure* came immediately to my mind). It was hard to figure out just how to make myself useful to teachers. I wanted to feel needed—probably a mistake. This is all intertwined with learning the culture of a new school, learning not to take sides in issues between teachers and administrators (my sympathies were heavily on the side of the teachers), and learning parts of the curriculum I didn't know. I felt inadequate and stupid most of the year. As a brand-new staff developer, I found it extremely difficult to figure out how to prioritize what I felt needed to be done. I wasn't sure when to push and when to back off.
>
> —Suzanne

> The greatest challenge has been trying to figure out what to focus on to help the teacher grow. I'll watch a lesson or plan the lesson with the teacher and help teach the lesson or observe the lesson. Sometimes I get so overwhelmed thinking, "Where do I even begin?" If I just take one piece it's more of a Band-Aid. I see the way the lesson is going and all of the times throughout the lesson that I would've made other choices as a teacher. Each time they make a different

choice it gets them further and further away from the way the lesson could be taught.

—Charlene

One of the problems is that the teacher and I have really different management styles. I will not yell at children; she screams at them. It's a touchy situation because I'm trying to get them to the meeting area to listen and talk while she's screaming at them. I refuse to yell at them so there's this kind of tug and pull between us. She thinks I'm not getting them to do what she thinks is best, so she screams. It's awkward.

—Elizabeth

I have a big issue with feeling patronizing toward people. I have a tendency to talk. I know I need to listen more and talk less. Also I'm not always comfortable with the math—I feel more comfortable just talking it out with somebody. With a number of teachers, I feel it is a true collaboration. The fifth-grade teacher leader at one of my schools knew the curriculum better than I did. She's a great math teacher. I felt like it was dialogue back and forth. With some teachers I tried asking the questions, but I felt like I needed to be really careful about how I asked them. It was a school that, from what I understood, hadn't had continuity of staff developers. A lot of teachers didn't want somebody in their room and I felt like, especially for the first year, I had to tread really carefully. I feel like the one thing I did is open up a dialogue with a lot of people who didn't want anybody in their room and who didn't work with the curriculum too much.

—Debbie F.

Having what I need in the building is a challenge. I don't have a desk, I don't have file cabinets. I need a place. I need a file, a file cabinet, bookshelves, because so many times I'm talking to teachers and I'm thinking, "Oh, I have something that would work really well but it's at home and I'm not going to see them for another week." I don't have resources and that's frustrating to me. I don't have a computer, which is frustrating to me. I've managed to use the computers in different rooms. Another thing is not having access to the copy machines—for the teachers that's frustrating. That's the difference between my old job and this—I had one room with everything I needed. Teachers need things and coaches need to be able to give them things.

—Charlene

Expressing frustration is only healthy for a little while. It is important to then consider how to address challenges in creative ways that will ultimately build a community of learning professionals. We believe that means being a learner yourself and being willing to do what it takes to gain credibility, including finding out what you don't know and figuring out how to learn it.

Of course I tried to read all the units for every grade before the year started, but that is very much like undergrad work. You don't really learn anything until you get in the classroom and do it. Being in the classroom with the teachers is where I am learning the most. I have become a more thorough planner in the grades I never worked in. I believe that is because I had so many questions for the teachers about what the students could, would, and were doing, I was making them think more closely about their students while I learned. I was also relearning mathematics the way it should have conceptually been taught to me.

—Karen

You have to prove you could teach here [in someone else's classroom]. I really think that's the first thing. The other thing that's nice is, because I'm a teacher, they know that I'm not administrative in any way. So you can't be used to evaluate them. I think it's really important they know that you're a peer. You have to know the math—I mean you have to be knowledgeable. I think they find out very quickly if you don't know what you're talking about.

—Elizabeth

I have been working on keeping the modeling short, so the teacher has more control over management and the students have more time to work on the activity. Most of the time the teacher does the lesson and either I observe or I jump in to support her, but only if she asks. She prefers to teach the lessons and not observe me modeling. This is not a good model of staff development for her because she can benefit from more modeling. We have recently worked out a compromise in which she introduces the lesson, we work together when the students are working in small groups, and then I do the share. This is more of a team-teaching model.

—Jean

It takes awhile to earn trust from the people you work with, and it is essential for doing this work. I think I've learned to treat teachers with the same kind of respect I tried to give my students. I'm more aware that each teacher is working with different understanding and beliefs.

—Linda

The best thing that I do is always go back to the kids' work. If you can get the conversation away from personality things and just understand what the kids do, that seems to help. I say, "Let's just look at what they did." That's the best approach that I could find. The evidence doesn't lie. That, for me, is the biggest piece.

—Elizabeth

Acknowledging Progress

When you are in the middle of the storm, it is hard to imagine the calm. This is often how it feels when doing the messy, difficult, and uncharted work of professional development. Taking a step back and reflecting on what has been accomplished, what is improving, and what seems to be working is not only healthy—it is useful. It gives you both the courage to go on and ideas for next steps. Sometimes progress is found in a change of teacher attitude, a new enthusiasm, or better planning skills. It's like looking for signs of spring after a cold winter.

I have worked with the teacher for two years and during this time have seen a shift in classroom practice. Her questioning of students has become more process oriented. Questions such as "Why do you think so?" "How did you arrive at that answer?" and "Can someone explain it another way?" are now commonly heard in her class. Her positive rapport with her students creates a comfortable classroom environment.

—Charlene

He finally realized that kids were having a really hard time understanding the concept. And he got to the point where instead of getting angry at them, he thought maybe they're acting out because they feel so unsuccessful. So he rewrote stuff to make it easier for them. Definitely an improvement, but it's still pretty rough going.

—Debbie A.

One of the ways that my work has changed over the years is that I have been doing less modeling of math lessons than I did in the first two years. I think this reflects some of the progress that has been made schoolwide. More teachers are familiar with the curriculum, so they have a better vision of what a rich math discussion looks and sounds like. I am pleased that the more experienced teachers seem to be serving as resources for new teachers, and that at least some of the teachers plan lessons together from time to time.

—Nina

Seeing how much they're actually planning on their own. In some cases follow-up definitely happens. In other words, if we've done a lesson, when I come in the next week they're like, "Remember when they did this? Well then I did that and that." Or, "You can't believe what my kids did." When teachers start to give feedback about what happened between coaching sessions, I think that is progress. Also, teachers who for X number of years have been unwilling to go to workshops are now willing to go to workshops. Teachers actually seek me out when it is not our planning time or teachers who I don't work with have started to come and say, "Oh I did this, what do you think about it?" Teachers are more willing to participate in the dialogue.

—Debbie F.

Acknowledging Self-Growth

If coaches are to maintain a learning stance, they need to take time to reflect on what they have learned and celebrate and acknowledge their progress. In District 2 we sometimes dedicate part of a meeting to recognizing ourselves and each other.

> I have learned to look at the big picture more, and I guess it is because of working across the grades—you see more clearly the reasons why you are doing the specific things you are doing and try to bring that meaning and consciousness to your teachers.
>
> —Karen

> I've used the Guide on Core Issues for Lesson Design but I think at this point I've internalized many of those questions, and I find that with the new teachers in particular, going through that whole template is a little too time consuming. For example, the "What is mathematics" is always something that I talk to teachers about. I've been conscious of thinking about "What would Lucy say in this situation, or what would someone else whose style I like say in this situation?"
>
> —Sarah

> I think when you're in the middle of teaching you just get so bogged down on everything. You're sort of in the middle of this chaos. Now that I've stepped out of that, I look at a class from a different point of view. I think I try to be more specific with content; I think I have clearer content goals for each weekday unit. I really try to assess how kids are learning that content. I think I am just more specific about, you know, what the math is, what my goal is, how this question, activity, addresses that goal. I think I probably tear apart my lessons more than I had in the past. I think I had all of those pieces floating around in my head, but I don't think I was actually so specific in being very detailed about how I wanted the classes to go.
>
> —Charlene

It's interesting. As I'm reading the book [curriculum materials] I'm seeing the investigations building on each other so much more clearly. I plan out the investigations before we come together—you'll see all my Post-it notes on all the investigations. I saw the flow much clearer this year for the first time, which is really interesting because I've been using these materials for four years. I can take bigger pieces now, because I know the books. I can take investigation chunks and lay out the investigation, whereas other years, I took the lesson and found what came before and what came after—a little three-piece part. Now I can pull out the investigation and I can see the *whole* investigation and where it fits in the book.

—Elizabeth

Content-Focused Coaching can make a difference in the lives of children and teachers. If done well, it can be a catalyst for intelligent change and sustainable improvement in schools and districts. Content-Focused Coaching is one professional development practice that can contribute to building vibrant, robust learning communities in which everyone from superintendent to staff developer to principal to teacher is invested in becoming smarter about teaching and learning. Most important, the practice of Content-Focused Coaching is one way to ensure that meeting students' needs and challenging students remain at the core of professional development efforts.

Appendix: The Institute for Learning's Principles of Learning (Resnick & Hall 2001)

Organizing for Effort

An effort-based school replaces the assumption that aptitude determines what and how much students learn with the assumption that sustained and directed effort can yield high achievement for all students. Everything is organized to evoke and support this effort, to send the message that effort is expected and that tough problems yield to sustained work. High minimum standards are set and assessments are geared to the standards. All students are taught a rigorous curriculum, matched to the standards, along with as much time and expert instruction as they need to meet or exceed expectations.

Clear Expectations

If we expect all students to achieve at high levels, then we need to define explicitly what we expect students to learn. These expectations need to be communicated clearly in ways that get them "into the heads" of school professionals, parents, the community, and above all, the students. Descriptive criteria and models of work that meet standards should be publicly displayed, and students should refer to these displays to help them analyze and discuss their work. With visible accomplishment targets to aim toward at each stage of learning, students can participate in evaluating their own work and setting goals for their own effort.

(For an additional CD-ROM study tool for this principle, see also Resnick & Bill 2001.)

Fair and Credible Evaluations

If we expect students to put forth sustained effort over time, we need to use assessments that students find fair and that parents, community, and employers find credible. Fair evaluations are ones that students can prepare for: therefore, tests, exams, and classroom assessments—as well as the curriculum—must be aligned to the standards.

Fair assessment also means grading against absolute standards rather than on a curve, so students can clearly see the results of their learning efforts. Assessments that meet these criteria provide parents, colleges, and employers with credible evaluations of what individual students know and can do.

Recognition of Accomplishment

If we expect students to put forth and sustain high levels of effort, we need to motivate them by regularly recognizing their accomplishments. Clear recognition of authentic accomplishment is a hallmark of an effort-based school. This recognition can take the form of celebrations of work that meets standards or intermediate progress benchmarks enroute to the standards. Progress points should be articulated so that, regardless of entering performance level, every student can meet real accomplishment criteria often enough to be recognized frequently. Recognition of accomplishment can be tied to opportunity to participate in events that matter to students and their families. Student accomplishment is also recognized when student performance on standards-based assessments is related to opportunities at work and in higher education.

Academic Rigor in a Thinking Curriculum

Thinking and problem solving will be the "new basics" of the twenty-first century. But the common idea that we can teach thinking without a solid foundation of knowledge must be abandoned. So must the idea that we can teach knowledge without engaging students in thinking. Knowledge and thinking are intimately joined. This implies a curriculum organized around major concepts that students are expected to know deeply. Teaching must engage students in active reasoning about these concepts. In every subject, at every grade level, instruction and learning must include commitment to a knowledge core, high thinking demand, and active use of knowledge.

Accountable Talk^{SM}

Talking with others about ideas and work is fundamental to learning. But not all talk sustains learning. For classroom talk to promote learning it must be accountable—to the learning community, to accurate and appropriate knowledge, and to rigorous thinking. Accountable talk seriously responds to and further develops what others in the group have said. It puts forth and demands knowledge that is accurate and relevant to the issue under discussion. Accountable talk uses evidence appropriate to the discipline (for example, proofs in mathematics, data from investigations in science, textual details in literature, documentary sources in history) and follows established norms of good reasoning. Teachers should intentionally create the norms and skills of accountable talk in their classrooms.

(For an additional CD-ROM study tool see Michaels, O'Connor, Hall & Resnick 2002.)

Socializing Intelligence

Intelligence is much more than an innate ability to think quickly and stockpile bits of knowledge. Intelligence is a set of problem-solving and reasoning capabilities along with the habits of mind that lead one to use those capabilities regularly. Intelligence is equally a set of beliefs about one's right and obligation to understand and make sense of the world, and one's capacity to figure things out over time. Intelligent habits of mind are learned through the daily expectations placed on the learner. By calling on students to use the skills of intelligent thinking—and by holding them responsible for doing so—educators can "teach" intelligence. This is what teachers normally do with students from whom they expect much; it should be standard practice with all students.

Self-Managment of Learning

If students are going to be responsible for the quality of their thinking and learning, they need to develop—and regularly use—an array of self-monitoring and self-management strategies. These *metacognitive* skills include noticing when one doesn't understand something and taking steps to remedy the situation, as well as formulating questions and inquiries that let one explore deep levels of meaning. Students also manage their own learning by evaluating the feedback they get from others, bringing their background knowledge to bear on new learning, anticipating learning difficulties and apportioning their time accordingly, and judging their progress toward a learning goal. These are strategies that good learners use spontaneously and all students can learn through appropriate instruction and socialization. Learning environments should be designed to model and encourage the regular use of self-management strategies.

Learning as Apprenticeship

For many centuries most people learned by working alongside an expert who modeled skilled practice and guided novices as they created authentic products or performances for interested and critical audiences. This kind of apprenticeship allowed learners to acquire complex interdisciplinary knowledge, practical abilities, and appropriate forms of social behavior. Much of the power of apprenticeship learning can be brought into schooling by organizing learning environments so that complex thinking is modeled and analyzed, and by providing mentoring and coaching as students undertake extended projects and develop presentations of finished work, both in and beyond the classroom.

References

Aebli, H. 1951. Didactique psychologique. Application à la didactique de la psychologie de Jean Piaget [Psychological Didactics. Applications of Jean Piaget's Psychology to Didactics]. Neuchâtel, Switzerland: Delachaux & Niestlé.

———. 1981. Denken: das Ordnen des Tuns. Band II: Denkprozesse [Thinking: The Structurizing of Action. Volume II: Processes of Thinking]. Stuttgart, Germany: Klett-Cotta.

———. 1983. Zwölf Grundformen des Lehrens [Twelve Basic Forms of Teaching]. Stuttgart, Germany: Ernst Klett.

Anderson, R., and K. Snyder, eds. 1993. Clinical Supervision: Coaching for Higher Performance. Lancaster, PA: Technomic Publishing Company.

Brand, R., ed. 1989. Readings from Educational Leadership: Coaching and Staff Development. Alexandria, VA: Association for Supervision and Curriculum Development.

Bromme, R. 1992. Der Lehrer als Experte. Zur Psychologie des professionellen Wissens [The Teacher as Expert. On the Psychology of Professional Knowledge]. Bern, Switzerland: Huber.

Burns, M. 2001. About Teaching Mathematics: A K–8 Resource. Sausalito, CA: Math Solutions Publications.

Chapin, S. H., and A. Johnson. 2000. Math Matters: Understanding the Math You Teach. Sausalito, CA: Math Solutions Publications.

Collins, A., J. S. Brown, and S. Newman. 1989. "Cognitive Apprenticeship: Teaching the Craft of Reading, Writing, and Mathematics." In Knowing, Learning, and Instruction, ed. L. B. Resnick, 453–494. Hillsdale, NJ: Lawrence Erlbaum Associates, Inc.

Costa, A., and R. Garmston. 1994. Cognitive Coaching: A Foundation for Renaissance Schools. Norwood, MA: Christopher-Gordon Publishers, Inc.

Elmore, R. F. 2001. "Content-Focused Professional Development: An Issue of Policy and Practice in Large-Scale School Reform." Paper presented at the meeting of the American Educational Research Association. Seattle: Wa.

Fink, E., and L. B. Resnick. 2001. "Developing Principals as Instructional Leaders." Phi Delta Kappan 2001: 598–606.

Fosnot, C. T., and M. Dolk. 2001a. "Constructing Number Sense, Addition, and Subtraction." In Young Mathematicians At Work. Portsmouth, NH: Heinemann.

————. 2001b. Constructing Multiplication and Division. In *Young Mathematicians At Work*. Portsmouth, NH: Heinemann.

Fullan, M. G. 1995. "The Limits and the Potential of Professional Development." In *Professional Development in Education*, ed. T. R Guskey and M. Huberman, 258–267. New York: Teachers College Press.

————. 1999. *Change Forces: The Sequel*. Philadelphia, PA: Routledge Falmer Press, Taylor & Francis, Inc.

Grant, C. M., Nelson, B. S., Davidson, E., Sassi, A., Weinberg, A., & Bleiman, J. 2002a. *Lenses on Learning, Module 1: Instructional Leadership in Mathematics*. Parsippany, NJ: Dale Seymour Publications.

————. In press. *Lenses on Learning, Module 2: Teacher Learning for Mathematics Instruction*. Parsippany, NJ: Dale Seymour Publications.

————. 2002b. *Lenses on Learning, Module 3: Observing Today's Mathematics Classroom*. Parsippany, NJ: Dale Seymour Publications.

Hiebert, J., T. P. Carpenter, E. Fennema, K. C. Fuson, D. Wearne, H. Murray, A. Olivier, and P. Human. 1997. *Making Sense: Teaching and Learning Mathematics with Understanding*. Portsmouth, NH: Heinemann.

Huberman, M. 1995. "Networks That Alter Teaching: Conceptualizations, Exchanges, and Experiments." *Teachers and Teaching: Theory and Practice* 1 (2):193–211.

Joyce, B., and B. Showers. 1995. "Student Achievement Through Staff Development." *Fundamentals of School Renewal (2nd ed.)*. White Plains, NY: Longman.

Klafki, W. 1958. Didaktische Analyse als Kern der Unterrichtsvorbereitung [Didactic analysis as the core of preparation of instruction]. *Die Deutsche Schule* 50 (10): 450–471.

————. 1963. *Studien zur Bildungstheorie und Didaktik [Studies on the theory of "Education" and "Didaktik"]*. Weinheim, Germany: Beltz.

————. 1995. "Didactic Analysis As the Core of Preparation of Instruction (Didaktische Analyse als Kern der Unterrichtsvorbereitung). *Journal of Curriculum Studies* 27 (1): 13–30.

Kliman, M., S. J. Russell, T. Wright, and J. Mokros. 1998. "Mathematical Thinking At Grade 1." In *Investigations in Number, Data, and Space*, ed. B. Cory. White Plains, NY: Dale Seymour Publications.

Leinhardt, G. 1993. "On Teaching." In *Advances in Instructional Psychology*, ed. R. Glaser, 1–54. Hillsdale, NJ: Lawrence Erlbaum Associates, Inc.

Ma, L. 1999. *Knowing and Teaching Elementary Mathematics*. Mahwah, NJ: Lawrence Erlbaum Associates, Inc.

Michaels, S., M. C. O'Connor, and M. W. Hall with L. B. Resnick. 2002. *Accountable Talk: Classroom Conversation That Works*. (CD-ROM, E-Book Beta version 2.0.) Pittsburgh, PA: University of Pittsburgh, Learning Research and Development Center, Institute for Learning, <www.instituteforlearning.org>.

National Council of Teachers of Mathematics. 2000. *Principles and Standards for School Mathematics*. Reston, VA: National Council of Teachers of Mathematics.

Resnick, L. B. 1987. *Education and Learning to Think*. Washington, D.C.: National Academy Press.

Resnick, L. B. 1995a. From the bell curve to all children can learn. (Video-based lecture.) Pittsburgh, PA: University of Pittsburgh, Institute for Learning.

———. 1995b. "From Aptitude to Effort: A New Foundation for Our Schools." *Daedalus* 124 (4): 55–62.

Resnick, L. B., and M. W. Hall. 1998. "Learning Organizations for Sustainable Education Reform. *Daedalus* 127 (4): 89–118.

Resnick, L. B., and M. W. Hall. 2001. *The Principles of Learning: Study Tools for Educators*. (CD-ROM, version 2.0.) Pittsburgh, PA: University of Pittsburgh, Learning Research and Development Center, Institute for Learning, <www.instituteforlearning.org>.

Resnick, L. B., and S. Nelson-Le Gall. 1997. "Socializing Intelligence." In *Piaget, Vygotsky and Beyond*, eds. L. Smith, I. Dockrell and P. Tomlinson, 145–158. London: Routledge.

Resnick, L. B., and V. L. Bill. 2001. *Clear Expectations: Putting Standards to Work in the Classroom*. (CD-ROM, Beta version 1.0.) Pittsburgh, PA: University of Pittsburgh, Learning Research and Development Center, Institute for Learning, <www.instituteforlearning.org>.

Schön, D. 1987. *Educating the Reflective Practitioner: Toward a New Design for Teaching and Learning in the Professions*. San Francisco: Jossey-Bass.

Showers, B., B. Joyce, and B. Bennett. 1987. "Synthesis of Research on Staff Development: A Framework for Future Study and a State-of-the-Art Analysis." *Educational Leadership* 45 (3): 77–87.

Shulman, L. S. 1987. "Knowledge and Teaching: Foundations of the New Reform." *Harvard Educational Review* 57 (1): 1–21.

———. 1998. "Theory, Practice, and the Education of Professionals." *The Elementary School Journal* 98 (5): 511–526.

Staub, F. C. 1999. *Reflection on Content-Focused Coaching Dialogues*. Pittsburgh, PA, University of Pittsburgh, The Institute for Learning.

———. 2001. "Fachspezifisch-pädagogisches Coaching: Förderung von Unterrichtsexpertise durch Unterrichtsentwicklung" [Content-Focused Coaching in teaching: Fostering teaching expertise through long-term classroom-based assistance in design and enactment of lessons]. *Beiträge zur Lehrerbildung* 19 (2): 175–198.

Staub, F. C., and E. Stern. 2002. "The Nature of Teachers Pedagogical Content Beliefs Matters for Students Achievement Gains: Quasi-experimental Evidence from Elementary Mathematics." *Journal of Educational Psychology* 94 (2): 344–355.

Staub, F. C., L. West, and A. Miller. 1998. Content-Focused Coaching: Scaffolding Teaching and Reflection on Core Issues of Instructional Practice. Paper presented at the American Educational Research Association, San Diego, CA.

Stigler, J. W., and J. Hiebert. 1999. *The Teaching Gap*. New York: The Free Press.

Thomas, A. M. 1995. *Coaching for Staff Development*. Leicester, UK: The British Psychological Society.

Tierney, C., and M. Berle-Carman. 1998. "Fair Shares." In *Investigations in Number, Data, and Space,* ed. B. Cory. White Plains, NY: Dale Seymour Publications.

Tierney, C., M. Ogonowski, A. Rubin, and S. J. Russell. 1995. "Different Shapes, Equal Pieces." In *Investigations in Number, Data, and Space,* ed. B. Cory. White Plains, NY: Dale Seymour Publications.

Van Dijk, T. A., and W. Kintsch. 1983. *Strategies of Discourse Comprehension*. Orlando: Academic Press.

Westbury, I. 2000. "Teaching As a Reflective Practice: What Might Didaktik Teach Curriculum?" In *Teaching As a Reflective Practice: The German Didaktik Tradition*, ed. I. Westbury, S. Hopmann, and K. Riquarts, 15–39. Mahwah, NJ: Lawrence Erlbaum Associates, Inc.

Whitmore, J. 1992. *Coaching for Performance*. London: Nicholas Brealey Publishing.

Wilson, S. M., and J. Berne. 1999. "Teacher Learning and the Acquisition of Professional Knowledge: An Examination of Research on Contemporary Professional Development." *Review of Research in Education* 24: 173–209.

Further Readings

Ball, D. 1996. "Teacher Learning and the Mathematics Reforms: What Do We Think We Know and What Do We Need to Learn?" *Phi Delta Kappan* 77: 500–508.

Ball, D. L., and D. K. Cohen. 1999. "Developing Practice, Developing Practicioners: Toward a Practice-Based Theory of Professional Education." In *Teaching As the Learning Profession: Handbook of Policy and Practice,* ed. G. Sykes and L. Darling-Hammond, 3–32. San Francisco: Jossey Bass.

Burns, M. 2001. "Lessons for Introducing Fractions." In *Teaching Mathematics,* ed. T. Gordon. Sausalito, CA: Math Solutions Publications.

Carpenter, T. P., E. Fennema, M. L. Franke, L. Levi, and S. B. Empson. 1999. *Children's Mathematics: Cognitively Guided Instruction.* Portsmouth, NH: Heinemann.

Elmore, R. F. 1999–2000. "Building a New Structure for School Leadership." *American Educator* Winter 1999–2000: 8–13, 42–43.

Fosnot, C. T., and M. Dolk. 2001. "Constructing Fractions, Decimals, and Percents." In *Young Mathematicians At Work,* ed. V. Merecki and L. Peake. Portsmouth, NH: Heinemann.

Handal, G., and P. Lauvas. 1987. *Promoting Reflective Teaching: Supervision in Practice.* Milton Keynes, England: Open University Press.

Resnick, L. B., and T. K. Glennan. In press. "Leadership for Learning: A Theory of Action for Urban School Districts." In *School Districts and Instructional Renewal,* ed. A. M. Hightower, M. S. Knapp, J. A. Marsh, and M. W. McLaughlin. New York: Teachers College Press.

Russell, S. J., D. Schifter, V. Bastable, L. Yaffee, J. B. Lester, and S. Cohen. 1995. *Learning Mathematics While Teaching.* Newton, MA, Center for the Development of Teaching, Education Development Center, Inc.

Russell, S. J. 1997. *The Role of Curriculum in Teacher Development.* Cambridge, MA, TERC: 1–9.

Senge, P., A. Kleiner, C. Roberts, R. Ross, G. Roth, and B. Smith. 1999. *The Dance of Change: The Challenges to Sustaining Momentum in Learning Organizations.* New York: Doubleday.

Senge, P. N. Cambrom-McCabe, T. Lucas, B. Smith, J. Dutton, and A. Kleiner. 2000. *Schools That Learn: A Fifth Discipline Fieldbook for Educators, Parents, and Everyone Who Cares About Education.* New York: Doubleday.

Stein, M. K., M. S. Smith, and E. Silver. 1999. "The Development of Professional Developers: Learning to Assist Teachers in New Settings in New Ways." *Harvard Educational Review* 69 (3): 237–269.

Stein, M. K., M. S. Smith, and E. A. Silver. 2000. *Implementing Standards-Based Mathematics Instruction. A Casebook for Professional Development.* New York: Teachers College Press.

Tharp, R. G., and R. Gallimore. 1988. *Rousing Minds to Life. Teaching, Learning, and Schooling in Social Context.* Cambridge: Cambridge University Press.

Wheatley, M. J. 1999. *Leadership and the New Science: Discovering Order in a Chaotic World, 2nd ed.* San Francisco: Berrett-Koehler Publishers.